IN THE ARMS
OF ANGELS

Other Books by Joan Wester Anderson:

WHERE ANGELS WALK

WHERE WONDERS PREVAIL

AN ANGEL TO WATCH OVER ME

WHERE MIRACLES HAPPEN

JOAN WESTER ANDERSON

IN THE ARMS OF ANGELS

TRUE STORIES OF HEAVENLY GUARDIANS

LOYOLAPRESS.

CHICAGO

LOYOLAPRESS.

3441 N. ASHLAND AVENUE
CHICAGO, ILLINOIS 60657
(800) 621-1008
WWW.LOYOLABOOKS.ORG

Cover and interior design by Adam Moroschan

Library of Congress Cataloging-in-Publication Data

Anderson, Joan Wester.
  In the arms of angels : true stories of heavenly guardians / Joan Wester Anderson.
      p. cm.
  ISBN 0-8294-2040-1
  1. Angels. I. Title.
BT966.3.A53 2004
235'.3—dc22

2004002957

Printed in the United States of America
04 05 06 07 08 09 10 Versa 10 9 8 7 6 5 4 3 2 1

CONTENTS

CONTENTS

ACKNOWLEDGMENTS

Most books wouldn't be written without the help of some special people. I would like to acknowledge Jennifer Bayse Sander, who was the first to suggest that the time was right for an angel "update." I thank my agent, Joelle Delbourgo, and my editor, Joseph Durepos, for supporting Jennifer's inspiration and encouraging me along the way. Hugs also to my spouse, five offspring, three in-law kids, two grandchildren on earth and two already dancing with the angels. Your love and comfort surround me.

My thanks to readers who provided story leads for these pages or were able to fill in missing information. These sharp-eyed helpers include Nancy Blodgett of Palatine, Illinois; Nancee Donovan of Concord, New Hampshire; Mary Gray of Loveland, Colorado; Father John J. Hurley, pastor emeritus of St. Edna's parish in Arlington Heights, Illinois; Bob Johnston, online editor of Ripplemakers.com; Patricia Lipps of Yardley, Pennsylvania; Marie Schmidt of Carpentersville, Illinois; Julie Stumphauzer of Vermilion, Ohio; Dick Sullivan of Prospect Heights, Illinois; Sister Margaret Sullivan of Bath, Maine; Mary Beth and Wayne Cole of Bensalem, Pennsylvania, and Jim McGregor, the fire chief of Langley, British Columbia. A hug to author Sharon Kanna of Brookings, Oregon, who kindly shared her research with me.

Many words of appreciation to the gracious staffs at *Guideposts* magazine, New York, New York; Breakthrough Ministries, Lincoln, Virginia; Eternal Word Television Network, Birmingham, Alabama; the Vineyard Christian Fellowship, Anaheim, California; FOCUS Worldwide TV network, Metaire, Louisiana; the National Opinion Research Center, University of Chicago; and the Illinois State Police. I appreciate the technical help of members of the Fall of Saigon Marine Association, especially Ken Crouse, Kevin Maloney, and John Valdez; Michael Brown, the Webmaster of Spirit Daily; Marvin Moore, the editor of *The Sign of the Times;* Father Edward Pick, the pastor of St. Mary Star of the Sea parish in Longboat Key, Florida; and members of the Royal Canadian Mounted Police in Antigonish, Nova Scotia. As always, I am thankful for the efforts of the television and radio reporters and talk-show hosts who continue to air presentations on this topic.

Finally, a special note of gratitude to my readers and Web-site newsletter subscribers. You will never know how much your enthusiasm and support enrich my work and my life. You are the best.

INTRODUCTION

Make for yourself a new heart and a new spirit.

—EZEKIEL 18:31

Minutes after a bomb exploded in the Alfred B. Murrah Federal Building in downtown Oklahoma City on April 19, 1995, an Oklahoma woman phoned her sister in North Carolina to share the terrible news. "Oh!" her sister responded. "Can you imagine the angels that were there!"

It wasn't the kind of reaction one would expect in the midst of tragedy. Positive points of view, if there are any, usually emerge days or even months later, when dust has settled and people have moved beyond those first shocking moments. But the woman in North Carolina was seeing past the immediate horror into a spiritual realm, where even the most terrible happenings can be turned into good.

A few days later, the sisters heard about a woman who had been preparing food for a funeral luncheon at her church, west of

Oklahoma City, when the explosion occurred. She packed everything into her car to bring to the disaster scene, some twenty miles away, and as she drove onto an overpass, she had a view of the city. The hair stood up on the back of her neck. A gigantic cloud hung over the skyline, filled with hundreds of angels. She could clearly see them, all facing west, trailing long graceful wings, angels standing silent vigil over the ruins, confirming the revelation of the woman from North Carolina.[1]

A week after the World Trade Center explosions, word circulated that a trumpeter was playing at Ground Zero. A well-known photographer went to see for himself. In the eerie quiet of lower Manhattan, he could hear the notes as he approached a barricade. "The trumpeter stood in this urban canyon, illuminated by shafts of light caused by the smoke and dust." Who was he? In a place of such intense security, how could a lone musician be allowed behind police lines? Looking through his lens, framing the unlikely stranger amid the rays, the photographer realized that this was the photo of a lifetime. "But I couldn't depress the shutter," he said. He lowered the camera in defeat.

His colleagues reported the same phenomenon. Apparently, no one could snap a picture. "Maybe he's an angel," one suggested.

Mark Judelson, executive director of the Arts Council of Rockland, New York, was struck by this event and has written and performed a miniplay about it. Today he says, "I think the trumpeter was the angel Gabriel. With his music, he blessed this site of car-nage and taught us to accept loss."

Who could have imagined, a few decades ago, speaking of angels in such matter-of-fact conversations, allowing these heav-enly beings into our lives as mysterious intercessors, cherished companions, dependable protectors? Since the early 1990s—when angels made somewhat of a popular comeback—books, movies, stores, and even *Time* and *Newsweek* cover stories have focused on them not as myth but as a unique part of God's creation. Perhaps at this uncertain moment in history, they are needed more than ever. Peter Kreeft, an angelologist, author, and profes-sor at Boston College has observed that angels "appear on the brink of chaos, or catastrophe, or at least the threat of chaos or catastrophe. They are spiritual soldiers in the great cosmic jihad, the spiritual war between good and evil." Upon reflection, he says, it seems not such a strange idea. "Doesn't there often seem to be an unknown, unpredictable, invisible factor in history, espe-cially in times of physical or spiritual conflict, culture wars or spiritual warfare?" Perhaps the emergence of angels in the public consciousness during the 1990s was intended to be that "invisible factor," a merciful heavenly preparation for the difficult events that were to come.

Terrorist attacks on American soil and subsequent war have ended our peaceful complacency, perhaps forever. Church scandals have betrayed not only children but also the faithful in the pews. Corporate greed and personal corruption have seriously affected employees, stockholders, and retirees. The lack of moral principles in government; the misuse of the Internet; impoverished children in the midst of a society sated with "stuff"; a drug culture connected to more than 60 percent of the crimes in America; an entertainment industry pushing the limits of decency. Consider too the unnerving increase in natural disasters—the floods, tornadoes, and wildfires that can ruin lifetimes of labor in an instant—or the appearance of new and deadly diseases. We who were taught to maintain control over every aspect of our lives have discovered that such control is elusive, sometimes even impossible. In the past few years, nearly every institution in which we have placed our trust has faltered or collapsed, and the sense of loss can be overwhelming. Some have described it as a huge national mourning, with undercurrents of fear and grief even at the happiest of times. Many are poised for additional threats, wondering if God has simply abandoned us.

Yet this may be precisely the time when people can truly grow and change. Tragedy is a harsh refining process, but it creates new substance by tearing away the smug materialism and misdirected goals that may have driven us in an earlier time. People who rise from the ashes of despair will inevitably make the world a better place, but it is not an easy process. Elisabeth Kübler-Ross, the psychiatrist and author of the groundbreaking *On Death and Dying,* was perhaps the first to identify actual stages that people must experience and work through in order to handle bereavement in a healthy way. These stages, whether personal or global, include shock and denial, acknowledgement and intense sorrow, a period of disorganization and confusion, and finally, acceptance, moving on, and hopefully creating something positive out of the loss. Kenneth L. Pierpont, a pastor and director of the Character Inn Christian ministry in Flint, Michigan, says, "That is the way God usually works. He usually takes us through the valley of the shadow of death before we arrive at the table he has prepared for us. Some dark and difficult days are usually a part of God's good plan. That was true for the Lord Jesus himself. That will always be true for each of us."

Gospel musician Thomas Andrew Dorsey wrote the hymn "Precious Lord" while grieving the death of a loved one. "I am tired, I am weak, I am worn," the song laments. As Dorsey faced his sorrow, though, he said, "the Lord healed my spirit. I learned that when we are in our deepest anguish, when we feel farthest from God, this is when he is closest, and when we are most open to his restoring power." It can be the same for us.

As we travel this challenging journey, we are not alone. As we have learned, angels go alongside us. These marvelous beings, created at the beginning of time, are greater in power and might than any human—just two angels were sent to destroy all of Sodom and Gomorrah. Nonetheless, angels are concerned with every facet of our well-being; an angel even brought food to the prophet Elijah, advising Elijah that he would be of no use to the Lord if he was exhausted. Angels convey messages, warn us, and probably "run interference" with our consciences, prompting us to choose good over evil and strengthening us in times of temptation. Moreover, because they act only on God's authority and within his plan for us, God has promised us their aid: "See, I am sending an angel before you, to guard you on the way and bring you to the place I have prepared. Be attentive to him, and heed his voice. Do not rebel against him for . . . my authority resides in him" (Exodus 23:20–21 NAB). What a great gift. How foolish we would be to disregard it.

Of course, an angel's role is not always to lift our burden—recall that during Christ's suffering in the Garden of Gethsemane, an angel was sent to strengthen him, not to take the anguish away. Sometimes angels simply walk with us through our distress, bringing their glory and grace to bear on whatever hardships we face, helping us lift our eyes from the event at hand to the will of God *behind* the event. Perhaps what we need most in the present uncertain climate is the comfort of angels.

Stories about comfort abound. One hospital patient explains, "I felt a warmth come over me, as if angels were all around. In the midst of my fear, I was flooded with reassurance. Whatever tomorrow's surgery revealed, I would handle it."

Describing a chance encounter with an unusual street person, a teenager recounts, "His eyes were full of love. All my worry disappeared. I thought, *If God loves me, then why should I be upset about stuff I can't control, like bombs?*"

Such episodes of care, reassurance, blessing, and love are balm to our shaken spirits as we come to understand that God's promise is the only one worth counting on; his path is the true way to peace. Look back at the "coincidences" in your life with new eyes. Hasn't God been with you every step of your journey, even though you might not have recognized him? Hasn't he sent help and consolation in trying times, healed your broken heart, brought certain people into your life at the perfect moment? (Could some of those people have been angels in disguise?) Why should it be any different today than it was in biblical times?

The future holds excitement and opportunity. We may grow inwardly in new ways, emerge stronger, holier, and more interested in ministering to the needs of others than to ourselves. We may learn that the people in our lives are far more important than any personal achievement or possession. The Rabbi Harold Kushner once observed that all the complicated structures we spend so much time and energy creating are built on sand. "Only our relationships to other people endure. Sooner or later, the wave will come along and knock down what we have worked so hard to build up. When that happens, only the person who has someone's hand to hold will be able to laugh."

As the people whose stories are in this book have learned, we need not fear the future, for we have God's hand to hold. He has given us everything we need. Peace, hope, and comfort abide in his arms—and in the arms of angels.

GAGE'S GIRLS

And he dreamed, and behold a ladder set up on the earth,
and the top of it reached to heaven: and behold
the angels of God ascending and descending on it.

—GENESIS 28:12 KJV

December 24, 2001, started out like any other Christmas Eve for the townspeople of Moncton, New Brunswick. Last-minute shoppers mingled with church- and partygoers, and despite the rainy weather, a sense of anticipation filled the air. Twenty-four-year-old Tobi Gabriel and her three-year-old son, Gage, were part of the happy throng. Tobi, a resident of Toronto, had driven to her hometown of Moncton to spend the holidays with her son and her mother. Sometime around two o'clock in the afternoon on this gloomy Christmas Eve, Tobi grew restless. She bundled Gage in a warm sweater and sweatpants, grabbed her coat, and headed for the door. "We're going out to rent a movie, Mom. We'll be right back." Her mother, elbow-deep in food preparation, barely noticed.

Tobi and Gage never returned. At about eleven o'clock at night, Tobi's concerned mother phoned the police. It was almost Christmas, and brightly wrapped presents for her grandson were under the tree. Where could Tobi and Gage be?

It was a little early for the police to suspect foul play. Tobi had many friends to visit and perhaps Gage had fallen asleep while in someone's home and the adults didn't want to wake him. Despite a now-freezing rain, there had been no accidents reported. Tobi should have phoned, but she'd turn up. Such "missing persons" usually did.

Early the next morning, Linda Belliveau of the nearby town of Lower Cove went out to watch for her parents, whom she expected for Christmas-morning breakfast. It was dark and wet, and even more so along this shore area of the Bay of Fundy. "I was glad I had left the lights on all night after I'd returned from Midnight Mass," said Linda. The candles and manger scene were the only sources of illumination along the whole beach.

Despite the roar of the waves behind her, Linda thought she heard a cry, like that of a baby. Impossible. No children would be out on this frigid dawn. The cry sounded again, mournful and frightened. Linda says, "Somehow, I felt compelled to find out what it was."

Linda hurried toward the sound. Ahead of her, alongside the shore, she saw a strange shape. As she neared it, Linda gasped. It was a car, lying upside down in the sand, just a short distance from the surf.

Linda realized that the car had probably plunged off the steep side of a nearby cliff, an area of highway known for being dangerous. There had been plenty of ice last night. She quickened her step. Surely no one could have survived. Yet she kept hearing that little wail.

Suddenly, she made out a small figure on the sand, crawling toward her. It was a tiny child, scooting along on his elbows and weeping inconsolably. "Honey!" Linda ran to him. "How did you get here? What happened?" His clothes were soaked, and she tore off her own coat to wrap it around him.

The child clutched her. "Mommy," he whispered.

In the growing dawn, Linda saw what must be a body, floating face down in the water. It was this child's mother. Was there any hope for her? Linda had been picking up the little boy, but she paused. "I'll go and help your mommy," she told him. But the child tightened his grip on her. "No!" he cried. "Don't go there."

She wondered what terrors he had been through during the night, what he had seen, how long he had been on this lonely, freezing beach. "What's your name, sweetheart?" she asked.

"Gage Gabriel. I lost my ducky boots."

"We'll buy you another pair," Linda promised as she lifted him up once more. "I'll bring you back to my house and get you warm."

She saw her parents' car pulling up. She decided that her dad could take charge of the scene because from the way Gage was clinging to her, she knew she'd be going to the hospital with him. This was going to be a Christmas morning like no other.

Tobi Gabriel had died on impact. Preliminary investigations found that she had not been wearing her seat belt and that drugs or alcohol had not been involved. She had probably lost control of the car when she hit a patch of frozen sea spray. At least one passing driver had noticed skid marks on the road at about ten o'clock at night, but police speculated that the accident had occurred several hours earlier because Tobi had been visiting friends and had left for home with Gage sometime after six.

Questions lingered about Gage. It appeared as if he had been lying down in the backseat, asleep. Since the car had rolled over at least twice—and shattered glass had flown—shouldn't he have sustained more severe injuries than a bump on the head and bruised hips? How had he suffered only frostbitten toes during an estimated twelve hours of below-freezing temperatures, wearing just a wet sweater and knit pants? Had he slept or been unconscious for part of that time? Had he stayed in the car or crawled along the beach? Linda was glad she had left her lights on all night. "Although he couldn't tell us, I like to think that perhaps he saw Jesus and the shepherds and wasn't so afraid."

Perhaps even more miraculous, according to Sergeant Dale Bogle of the Royal Canadian Mounted Police, was that Gage didn't drown. "Usually, during high tide, the area where the car was found should be under water." Since Gage was on the beach during a complete tidal cycle, no one knows why the water did not come in all the way to the cliff that night.

Most of it is a mystery, but not all of it. Sergeant Bogle was visiting Gage in Amherst Hospital just a few hours after his rescue, asking him some gentle questions, when the little boy looked up. "I saw two girls," he announced matter-of-factly.

The officer was taken aback. "You did? Where?"

"Standing in the water, next to Mommy," Gage answered. "Their dresses were white."

"Did they talk to you?"

"No. They smiled at me. They smiled at me all night, until that other lady came."

Gage reported the same story to his dad, and later his grandmother, and added that the girls seemed to have wings. "Were they ladies?" his grandmother asked.

"No," Gage was definite. "Girls!"

How could a child of three come up with something like this? Sergeant Bogle voiced this question as he shared the story with his fellow officers. They had no answers. No one had interviewed Gage

yet; there had been no chance to plant such an idea in his mind—
if anyone would. No one was sure that Gage had ever been told
about angels.

Gage now lives with his father; his grandfather calls him "a gift
from God." He seems happy and well adjusted and rarely speaks of
that difficult night. For those who care about him, there remains just
a little hint of mystery, of wonder, of joy, in the midst of loss—and
the hope that the "girls" who comforted him on that dark and lonely
beach will watch over him forever.

GUARDIAN IN THE TOWER

Not only do baptized Christians receive an angel,
but every member of the human race.

—Saint Thomas Aquinas

It started as an ordinary day for Genelle Guzman, a then twenty-nine-year-old administrative assistant for the New York Port Authority. For the past nine months, she had been working at a computer on the sixty-fourth floor of the north tower of the World Trade Center. She would have liked a more stimulating job, but, born and raised in Trinidad, Genelle was in the United States on a nonimmigrant visitor's visa, which had expired. This certainly limited her job choices; if anyone found out, she could be deported.

Genelle was the youngest daughter of thirteen children, three of whom had died as babies. The family was poor, and her father was strict, and by the time Genelle was eighteen, she had left home to work in Port of Spain, the capital city of Trinidad. "I wanted independence," she explains. Although Genelle is naturally shy, there was something about the nightlife there that made her feel confident and alive, and she even became a "party girl." Later, Genelle gave birth to a baby daughter, Kimberly. In 1998, more adventure beckoned, and Genelle gave custody of Kimberly to the baby's father and moved to New York. She had relatives there, and she would live with a sister in Queens while she looked for a job. However, the shabby neighborhood and the noise of the city disturbed her, and soon she returned to Trinidad. A short time later, Genelle's mother died of ovarian cancer.

"I had always *said* I believed in God, but when Mom died, I wondered where he was." Genelle was angry with the God she barely knew, wondering why her mother, so faithful to him, had had such a difficult life. Eventually, though, anger turned to indifference. Religion seemed superfluous, even an impediment to the life Genelle was now living. She resumed her "party girl" lifestyle and was often out until dawn.

Genelle met Roger McMillan at a carnival in Trinidad, and it was instant attraction. She went back to New York in 1999 to pursue a relationship with him, and they lived together in Brooklyn. They assumed they would marry eventually, but as Genelle says, "I was still busy partying. I didn't want too much pressure on my relationship."

Genelle was aware, however, that her lifestyle was missing something indefinable but vital. Twice she and Roger had attended services at the Brooklyn Tabernacle, an evangelical congregation. Genelle was intrigued by one of the lessons, which emphasized "If you let God lead you, he will." What would that be like? To stop searching and just follow the lead of someone who loved you more than anything? This God had taken her mother away, though, and to join Brooklyn Tabernacle, she and Roger would have to change the way they lived. She decided that change wasn't worth the price. Neither she nor Roger had joined the congregation.

One morning at work, as she booted up her computer, Genelle stuck her head into a few cubicles to greet some of her coworkers. One of them, Susan, admired Genelle's gold braids, which Genelle and some of her cousins had done that Saturday. Just as Susan turned away to answer the phone, everyone in the office heard a loud bang, and the building shook. "What was that?" Genelle murmured as she hurried to the window. Stunned, she watched as bits and pieces of paper and debris fell through the air. The fire alarm rang, and a moment later the public-address system announced that an airplane had hit the upper floors and that people should stay put and not panic. Everyone was stunned. What kind of plane? How? Most ignored the instructions, grabbed their belongings, and fled. In a moment, just fifteen employees were left. Again there was an announcement that those in the building should stay where they were.

Another friend of Genelle's, Rosa, had just phoned her sister, and Genelle followed suit. She left a message on Roger's answering machine: "Honey, I'm staying in the building. I guess we have to wait until someone comes to get us out. I love you." She also phoned her cousins. They were bordering on hysteria.

"Get out of there! Leave now!" they told her, describing the scene on television. But the stairwells were filled with smoke, and the elevators had stopped. How could she get out alone?

Meanwhile, firefighters had arrived at the base of the north tower, their hoses putting out flames on some of the people who were exiting. Crews headed into the building and a moment later heard the sounds of a second plane approaching. Within seconds, that plane hit the south tower. Thousands of people were trapped, but the firefighters were ordered out of both unstable buildings. Most of them turned back.

On the sixty-fourth floor, Genelle and her fourteen colleagues also heard the second crash. The ceiling shook, the air around them was getting hot, and smoke seeped ominously under the closed doors. "That's it!" one of the men shouted. "We're walking down!" Rosa and Genelle grabbed each other's hands and followed the group to stairway B. It was less smoky than they had anticipated, and a wave of optimism filled them. Genelle phoned her cousin again and then Roger. This time he answered. He was waiting on a corner just a few blocks away, hoping that Genelle had managed to get out. "I'll meet you there!" he told her. "Hurry!" It was just ten o'clock in the morning, more than an hour since the first plane had struck.

At first the trek went well. Rosa and Genelle clung to each other, and by the fortieth floor, when they met some firefighters taking a break, their confidence grew. On the thirtieth floor another rescue worker reassured them that they would be fine. (These men either had not heard or had not heeded the order to retreat and would die in the building's collapse.) Genelle recalls counting the flights of stairs with Rosa: "Twenty, nineteen, eighteen. I was wearing a new pair of high-heeled shoes and my feet hurt. When we reached the next landing, I stopped to take my shoes off." Just then there was a roar—like a locomotive coming straight at them. The floor shifted, and part of a wall fell toward Rosa and Genelle, separating the women from each other. Dust filled the air, steel beams crashed, and cement was pulverized as people hurtled down flights of stairs. Then the lights went out. An eerie calm descended.

Genelle, attempting to crawl downward, had been trapped by falling chunks of cement. Now her head was pinned between two concrete pillars, her arms above her head, her legs under debris. "Help!" she cried out. "Is anyone there? Rosa?" No one answered. Genelle did not know it, but her building had collapsed and she had been the only survivor in this area.

Slowly, Genelle took stock. "My right leg was buried up to the thigh in rubble, and my toes were numb." Perhaps worse was the worry over what had happened outside. Had New York City been hit by a bomb? Were her loved ones alive? Would she die here, never being able to tell them that she loved them? As panic edged closer, she closed her eyes. For the first time in many years, she thought about God. She hadn't been a very faithful daughter of his, she knew. But from what she remembered from her mother's faith, she wasn't alone in this terrible place. God knew where she was— and he was here too. She began to pray.

Time passed; as the dust settled, Genelle saw a thin shaft of light somewhere ahead. Was that an exit? If so, where were the rescue workers? How would anyone find her if they didn't check this area? She heard nothing. As the light slowly faded, Genelle prepared to spend the night in complete darkness. She pleaded to God for him to stay by her side.

Genelle couldn't know that the scene somewhere above her was one of pandemonium. Smoke billowed from the pile of rubble that was once the World Trade Center; gigantic beams lay everywhere, and sirens screamed. Shocked and bleeding people wandered aimlessly, while others ran for their lives. "There was a sense of crazed panic, people fighting to save lives, firehoses cascading all over the place," said one eye witness. Thousands of people remained missing. Genelle was one of them.

Eventually, in the collapsed stairwell, the little ray of light returned, and Genelle knew morning had arrived. Drifting in and out of consciousness, she also knew that her life was ebbing away. "All feeling in my right leg was gone now, and I didn't think I could go too much longer without water." Still, she sensed the presence of Someone who truly cared about her. "God," she prayed, "please send me a sign that I'm going to get out of here. Or that if I don't, you'll be there to meet me."

Suddenly—was it true?—Genelle heard a muffled sound. "Hello!" she cried out, her voice hoarse and raspy from the dust. "Is anyone there?" There was movement, as if other people had entered the area. "I'm here!" she cried. "Can you hear me?" No one answered.

Genelle's hand was still stuck above her head, but maybe she could attract some attention. Frustrated, she tried to wave, and suddenly she felt someone take hold of her hand, holding it in a warm and reassuring grip. "You're going to get out of here," a male voice told her. "Don't be afraid."

"Oh, thank God!" Genelle could hardly believe it. "Where did you come from? What's your name?"

"I'm Paul," the gentle voice answered. "I'm just ahead of the rescue team. They're coming to get you. I'll stay here with you."

Holding on as hard as she could, Genelle tried to open her eyes so she could see Paul's face. "But for some reason, my eyes just wouldn't open." However, Paul was right—soon she could hear men's voices. "I'm shining a light down," someone called. "Can you see it?"

"No!" she called back, still unable to see anything. She used one hand to knock the staircase above her with a piece of concrete. The rescuers were definitely getting closer, but whenever they moved wreckage, fear surged through her—would there be another collapse? Paul seemed to know how she felt and would give her other hand a squeeze. Sensing her terror, he soothingly told her more than once: "It's going to take a while, but I will stay with you. You're going to be fine."

An eternity passed, and finally she heard two firemen above her, digging debris away from her leg, calling for others to send down a stretcher. "We've got her!" one shouted. As they reached her, in the confusion and joy of the moment, Genelle let go of Paul's hand, letting the others lift her onto the stretcher. It was 12:30 P.M. She had spent twenty-six hours buried underground, and she would be the last survivor pulled from the wreckage. Crowds cheered as she was carried to an ambulance. "I noticed that it was a sunny day, and I could open my eyes now. I wondered why I had not been able to open them and look at Paul." She had not seen him yet and didn't want to forget his name. When Roger arrived at the hospital, the very first thing she told him was to write it down. She would never be able to repay Paul for the care and comfort he brought to her during this terrible time, but she would try.

Roger had assumed he was being summoned to the hospital to identify Genelle's body. When he realized that he had not lost her after all, he suggested (through tears) that they get married. Genelle agreed. She had been given a new chance at life, she told him, and this time she would do it God's way.

Since then, Genelle has faced many challenges. She endured several surgeries on her crushed right leg (however, she no longer needs a leg brace, despite the medical prognosis that she would always use one). Psychologically, Genelle may not have completely worked through her fear and loss yet, but she is not depressed. Her legal problems have ended; the U.S. Immigration and Naturalization Service has decided not to prosecute illegal immigrants who were victims of this attack against America. Genelle is now a wife and a faithful member of the Brooklyn Tabernacle—she was baptized there shortly after she and Roger married. She is remarkably humble, quick to point out that she is not anyone special, just a child who has given her life to God—and she knows that this commitment does not mean a perfect life but one brimming with the "peace that passes all understanding." She does not believe that her rescue was about luck. "It's about God having a plan. And he will reveal it to me someday."

Only one loose end remains. At Christmas time, some of the firemen who rescued her came to visit her at home. She thanked them all, and then asked which one was Paul. "Paul?" the men looked at one another.

"Paul," Genelle said. "The one who found me first, the one who held my hand. He was just ahead of the rescue team."

The men shuffled and shook their heads. They knew every member of that squad, all the firemen who were currently searching for survivors. There was no one named Paul in any of those groups, and there had definitely been no one ahead of them when they rescued her.

Genelle believes that God did indeed send her a sign that all would be well, a sign in the form of an angel. For that reason, she is determined to make the most of her life and to regard it as a gift. "Those hours in the building turned out to be a wake-up call so I could get my life in order. If I had it to do over, I wouldn't change a thing."

COMFORT FROM BEYOND

∘◦⦕∞⦖◦∘

It was a quiet Sunday morning at Our Lady of Consolation Catholic Church in Callahan, Florida. No more than eighty people were attending Mass, but the church was so tiny that most of the pews were filled. To Jackie Hall, everything seemed normal as she gazed around the sunny space. Who among her neighbors here would have guessed that, despite Jackie's calm exterior, her mind and heart were in torment? Jackie was thinking seriously of committing suicide.

It is difficult, perhaps, for those who have never been clinically depressed to understand what a tremendous toll this illness takes on a person's mind and soul. Even people with strong spiritual faith can succumb to unbelievable feelings of sadness and, often, the unreasonable fear that depression and chronic pain create. Jackie had suffered from back problems for many years as a result of a car accident. She had recently given up a retail job she enjoyed in order to have fusion surgery. Her rehabilitation had been long and arduous, but she was still not well enough to go back to work or even to resume normal living. "I felt useless," she says. Her husband and children were at a loss to help her change from a morose and withdrawn woman back into the gracious, outgoing person they remembered. No one realized just how dark Jackie's thoughts had become recently.

For the previous few days, Jackie had been "getting ready," packing up family photos and organizing records, giving away certain possessions—all actions that are symptomatic of an impending suicide. On Sunday, she had awakened feeling especially fragile. Perhaps Mass would be her last outing. How she longed to feel God's love for her, his support! Even though she had often prayed to be delivered from despair, the answers had not come. Now the emotional pain was closing in on her. She could bear it no longer, and there seemed no other way out.

"When we arrived at church, I knelt and prayed with all my heart. I told God how much I loved him and begged him to guard me against whatever was happening to me." She needed a sign, just a little hint of reassurance or comfort. Once again, God seemed silent.

Several pews back and across the aisle, Judy Davies also knelt in prayer. She usually attended Sunday Mass at another church, the parish at which her son went to grade school, but today she had dropped into Our Lady of Consolation. Because the parish was so small, she usually knew everyone there.

However, this morning Judy noticed a woman just in front of her. She didn't know her, but as Mass began, something about the woman caught Judy's attention. What was it? The woman seemed sad, but she wasn't behaving unusually, just kneeling and praying. "I sensed a presence there. It's hard to describe, but the longer I looked, the more I seemed to see light around her, like an aura." The cloudlike glow was particularly strong behind the woman, as if some kind of force was protecting her. But from what? There was no danger in this peaceful church. Judy was even more astonished when she realized that no one else was reacting to this strange light. Was she the only one who could see it?

"I tried to keep my thoughts on the Gospel and the homily, but my eyes kept drifting to her, to see if the aura was still there. It was."

By the time Mass ended, the apparition had faded. Judy was in a quandary. Should she stop the woman and tell her about it? "Things like this are always hard to do," Judy says. "You don't want others to think you're strange. But I felt that I had to tell her." Judy followed the woman out and tapped her on the shoulder. When the woman turned, Judy plunged into her message.

"You are truly blessed," she said earnestly. "I saw a glow all around you during Mass. It looked like an angel was looking over your shoulder, protecting you. I just had to tell you!"

An angel! Jackie was almost speechless as she stared at the woman. "Well, thank you," she murmured politely and watched as Judy turned away. But her thoughts were racing. An angel, watching over her, caring for her? Could this be the sign she had asked God to send? Suddenly, she felt an enormous weight begin to lift and a small stirring of hope. Tears filled her eyes. She turned to her husband. "I need help. I want to live."

Jackie's life changed quickly. She found an effective medication and began to feel more like herself. One day at a meeting, she heard herself volunteering to visit a cancer patient in her parish, something unlike any activity she had ever participated in. It was the start of what would become a visitor program, ministering to the sick and the shut-ins in the neighborhood. The program became extremely popular, and after some consideration, Jackie agreed to become its director. Gradually, she came to understand that her own suffering had prepared her for this kind of ministry; in God's eyes, there had been a purpose for it all. She had developed a wellspring of patience and tenderness for others in need, and she was constantly amazed and grateful when her work bore fruit.

Four or five years passed. Jackie improved dramatically, became a grandmother several times, and considered each day a blessing. There was just one mystery left: who was the woman who had brought her the reassuring news that critical morning in church? And would she even recognize her if they were to meet again? Jackie longed to thank her, to ask how she could have known. . . .

One evening, Jackie attended a parish meeting, and a visitor asked the group a question about the Catholic church's teaching on angels. The host answered the question, and then Jackie spoke up. "I have an angel story. In fact, I think an angel saved my life!" As the audience sat transfixed, Jackie described her illness and that desperate morning when she almost gave up. "I haven't seen that woman since, even though our parish is small. I sometimes wonder if she was an angel in disguise."

From the back of the room, a woman spoke into the silence. "No," she said hesitantly, "I think it was me!"

Jackie gasped as Judy stood up. Both recognized each other and then embraced as the rest of the group wiped away tears. How had they failed to become acquainted during the last several years? Neither had an answer. God's timing is perfect, and he had started a chain reaction of faith that became an example to the entire parish.

Jackie and Judy have remained in touch and see each other every Sunday morning. "Our eyes often meet during Mass, and we share a smile from across the church," Judy says. She is enormously grateful that she took a risk and reached out to Jackie on that important morning. "Call it instinct, intuition, or a sign from God, but if someone feels the presence of the Lord—through his angel messengers—that person should share it."

We should also respond to any inner urge to pray, for a person or situation, even if we don't know all the details. Such a process is called *intercessory prayer.* A recent example of this is the experience of the trucker Ron Lantz, who, in October 2002, felt suddenly compelled to organize a prayer service for America, for "an end to evil in our country" and for the arrest of the snipers who were then terrorizing the Washington, D.C., area. Ron used his CB radio to contact other truckers, and more than fifty came to a prearranged stop near Baltimore on October 16 to pray.

Just a week later, Lantz was driving on a highway not too far from where the prayer meeting had taken place. Again, he had an urge to pull off into a rest area. There he saw a parked car matching the description of the sniper's vehicle. He dialed 911, and then pulled his rig across the exit just in case the two men sleeping in the car awakened and tried to escape. They did not, and a terrible siege of panic and fear finally ended. Ron was thrilled but not surprised. As do Jackie and Judy, Ron has always understood the power of prayer.

A BLESSED PLACE

And the things of this world will grow strangely dim,
In the Light of His glorious grace.
—"TURN YOUR EYES UPON JESUS," HYMN

Marsha Wood left her home one May afternoon in Maggie Valley, North Carolina, to pick up her husband. He worked in Cherokee, and Marsha had made the ten-mile drive hundreds of times. She used Highway 19, a two-lane, curvy road with steep drop-offs, which is also the connection to the Great Smoky Mountains National Park. The weather was beautiful, and she was enjoying the scent of spring flowers as she approached a sharp curve and braked. Nothing happened. Looking down, Marsha realized that her brake pedal had fallen off!

"Panic hit, and I tried vainly to gear it down." There was a camping area just ahead, Black Rock, and perhaps she could ease into that spot. Instead, the vehicle accelerated. "I blew my horn and flew around approaching cars—it's a miracle that I didn't hit anyone head-on." Marsha's mind raced. What could she do? The car was going faster and faster, and another sharp curve was approaching. Without warning, she slammed head-on into the side of the mountain.

"I crashed through the windshield, and then bounced back into the car. It seemed like a dream, but it was all too real. I realized that my left leg was dangling, and it must be broken, but at least no one else had been hurt." She needed to lie down, and she sank sideways into the passenger seat. The car seemed to be full of light. Was she unconscious? Was she dying?

Hands cradled her head, and a sweet female voice behind her spoke: "Lie still. You're badly hurt." Marsha realized she was still in the car, her feet against the driver's door, her head hanging out of the open passenger door. "Then a man with the most beautiful black hair and beard pulled open the driver's side door and began to examine my leg." She heard him talking, apparently on a phone to the paramedics, advising them to get to the scene quickly, saying that Marsha was losing a lot of blood and had possible spinal injuries.

The woman behind her spoke to the man, who was apparently a police officer. "Don't give her a ticket," she said. "This wasn't her fault—she did everything she could to stop the crash, and not hurt anyone." She mentioned the broken brake pedal and other precrash details. In a daze, Marsha listened. How did this woman know so much about the accident, and where had she come from? Suddenly in the midst of her pain, Marsha was filled with joy. This woman must be her guardian angel! "I tilted my head backward, taking a chance with my spine, but I had to see her!" The woman, from the waist up, came into view. "She was lovely, with beautiful blue eyes and blonde hair and hands that made you feel that everything was going to be all right. I will never forget the sight of her!"

Paramedics came, and eventually Marsha reached the Cherokee Indian Hospital, where she was examined. She had life-threatening injuries, including a broken leg, nose, and teeth; cracked ribs and sternum; and a bruised heart. The doctors decided to send her to the intensive-care unit at Mission Memorial in Asheville.

Suddenly, Marsha felt herself being lifted out of her body. "I looked down and saw them working on me. Then I began to look around, and there were angels everywhere, and a glorious light." It was peaceful, warm, and joy-filled in that place, and Marsha did not want to leave. But the light spoke, telling her that there was more on Earth for her to do, that she must go back.

Marsha awakened on the table. Her heart had stopped, and hospital workers had restarted it with the electric paddles. "But I knew that the Lord had done it. My time was not yet." In fact, when Marsha reached the Asheville hospital, she overheard personnel phoning her family members. "They did not expect me to live until daybreak. But as I lay there, I knew they were wrong. The voice I had heard had told me that I had more to do." As the weeks passed, even Marsha's physician said that her survival was a miracle.

Later, officers at the scene told Marsha that the rear end of her car was half on the road, half dangling over a deep ravine. With the car at that angle, no young woman could have stood or knelt outside the passenger door to hold Marsha's head; there was simply no ground there to support anyone. What, then, did the bearded police officer see when he got to the scene? (And why did he easily fling open the driver's door when it later took four men and several crowbars to pry Marsha from the wreckage?) These are questions that Marsha has never been able to answer. "But I believe I saw one and possibly even two angels at that site," she says today. "When people think of angels, they think flowing robes and halos. But in the Bible, they also look like ordinary people. Why not today?"

It's interesting to note that, like Marsha, the majority of those who have undergone near-death experiences say that they've encountered angels along the way. Apparently, these wonderful beings attend most journeys from this life into the next, no matter whether the transition appears peaceful or traumatic to those left behind. For example, monks who lived in the monastery with the recently canonized Italian priest Saint Pio often heard heavenly music drifting through the halls but could not identify its source. The priest matter-of-factly explained that the singing came from angels, who were escorting souls into heaven. On another occasion, a British researcher spoke with a woman who had sent her six-year-old son upstairs "to tell Grandpa it's time for dinner." The boy returned, reporting that he could not open the bedroom door all the way because the room was filled with angels. When his mother went up to check, she found that Grandpa had just died.

As far back as 1892, the Swiss scientist Albert Heim, who studied death and near-death experiences, concluded that the process of dying "is far more frightening to onlookers than it is for the dying themselves." It seems that despite the circumstances, the death experience begins with a sense of well-being and soon culminates in a feeling of ecstatic joy.

While watching the events of September 11, the songwriter Dave Allott was particularly sorrowful over those who had fallen or jumped from the buildings. How had they felt? What terror had gone through their minds? Suddenly, Dave "heard" song lyrics in his mind, somehow assuring him that these people were not aware of any pain or fear, that instead angels had surrounded them. Dave used the lyrics to write the song "Hand in Hand":

> As hand in hand
> We leave this life together . . .
> Hand in hand
> As angels lift us up upon their wings
> I hear them sing.

And the world seems far away
As the darkness turns into the brightest day.[2]

Such observations can bring much healing to survivors. As we mourn, especially victims of crime or accidents, we can believe that at the end angels shielded them from the violence and chaos and brought them to a place of safety and love. "This spiritual encounter has never left me," Marsha Wood says. "I truly look forward to the day when I can again enter that blessed world and not have to return."

STRANGER ON THE TRAIN

The angels . . . regard our safety, undertake our defense,
direct our ways and exercise a constant solicitude
that no evil befalls us.
—JOHN CALVIN

I t had been an exhilarating experience, Pastor Cecilio Bermudez mused as the Atlanta commuter train bounced its way along. Imagine! More than forty thousand clergy of all denominations from all parts of the country together over Valentine's Day weekend for the first Promise Keepers Clergy Conference in history—and he was a part of it! Not wanting to miss a single moment of praise or worship or any of the presentations, Cecilio and his three companions had gone all day without even taking time to eat. Now their stomachs were starting to growl, and they hoped to be back at their motel, and in its restaurant, very soon.

All four of the pastors were from the Southwest, but Cecilio was the only Hispanic, and he barely spoke English. At his First Baptist Church in Los Fresnos, Texas, he served primarily Spanish-speaking Americans. He was a gentle and humble man who had never been this far from the security of home. Cecilio was feeling rather vulnerable, especially because the train was crowded, and the four men were not sitting together. Cecilio kept George, a fellow pastor who was sitting ahead of him, in constant view. When George got up to exit, Cecilio would too. In the meantime his thoughts drifted to his wife (had she discovered the valentine he had left for her?), his grown son who lived nearby, and his beloved parishioners. How thrilled he would be to get back to familiar surroundings and tell them about this stirring rally!

All seats were taken now, and passengers were swaying in the aisle as the train rumbled on. Suddenly, a large man blocked Cecilio's glimpse of George. The train slid to a stop, the doors opened, then closed again before Cecilio could get a clearer view. Where was George? Still in his seat? And the other two pastors? Cecilio attempted to see around the crowd. Another stop, and doors slid opened again. Some laughing travelers boarded, one carrying a Valentine balloon bouquet that made it even more difficult to see. There was a break in the crowd, and Cecilio craned his neck to catch sight of George. But George wasn't there. None of his companions appeared to be on the train.

The crowd closed up again, and Cecilio began to panic. His friends must have left the train, assuming that he was just behind them. The doors opened and shut again. He was lost in a strange city more than a thousand miles from home, he didn't speak much English, and he had forgotten the name and address of his motel! Cecilio prayed, "Lord, please help me." It was the only prayer he could think to say. He sat silently, as the train continued its journey, stopping and starting, the crowd thinning, his friends farther and farther behind. What should he do? How could he make himself understood, if he could even *find* a friendly face?

When the train stopped again, Cecilio felt an inner nudge. *Get off here.* Obediently, he exited and sat, cold and hungry, on a concrete bench. Was God going to send him more directions?

Not at first. Gradually, Cecilio noticed that at the station, trains ran on three aboveground levels. He felt certain he was to go to the ground-level tracks, and again he obeyed. When a train came, he boarded. The train was almost deserted. As Cecilio selected a seat and sat down, he noticed two large men wearing soiled work clothes and talking loudly. Weaving and leering, they were obviously drunk. They stumbled down the aisle to the seat exactly across from Cecilio. Both sat down and stared at him strangely.

They were going to mug him, Cecilio realized. Given his small stature, he would be no match for them. He prayed even harder.

A tall, slender, white-haired gentleman, sitting several rows behind, was apparently aware of the situation. "Are you lost?" he asked Cecilio.

"Yes," Cecilio replied, turning.

The man moved a bit closer and smiled reassuringly. "Don't worry about it. I'll take you where you need to go."

He hadn't asked where Cecilio needed to go. He hadn't asked *any* other questions. Despite the large drunken men, Cecilio suddenly felt safe, even comforted. "Thank you," he answered.

The train went on, stopping several times. The intoxicated men apparently abandoned any criminal plans and eventually exited. Finally, when Cecilio had almost decided he would sleep on the train, the older man rose. "We'll get off here," he said. "Follow me."

Cecilio followed him and noticed that they were near the airport. Yes! This could be where the motel was—he remembered hearing planes overhead in his room. But his self-appointed guide moved confidently toward an elevator, and Cecilio hurried to catch up with him. In silence they rode to a lighted area on the first floor. Cecilio followed his rescuer through the long terminal and outside, across four lanes of traffic.

Finally, briskly approaching the last lane, the man pointed. "You see that red van? That van will take you where you need to go."

Somehow Cecilio understood. He stammered his thanks and walked toward the red van. It had a motel's name written on the side, but Cecilio couldn't be sure if it was the right one. He knocked on the driver's window. "Please take me to the motel," he said.

"I need to see your room key," the driver answered.

Cecilio shrugged. "I don't have one." He looked around for his rescuer, but the man was nowhere to be seen.

"Well, what's the name of your motel?"

"I don't know," Cecilio said. His heart sank. Was he to be stranded again?

The driver decided that the motel could sort out the problem. He let Cecilio sit in the rear area—along with all the luggage—and drove him and the other passengers back. As they entered the parking lot, Cecilio almost cheered. This was the right place!

The manager remembered him and provided another key. Cecilio took a shower and lay down to read his Bible as he waited for his friends. They were surely still looking for him but would return eventually. As he waited, his thoughts turned to the mysterious stranger on the train. From the moment the two had met, the night had taken on a mystical quality. Why had the man spoken to Cecilio in the first place? The two had not been sitting that close to each other. Why had he assumed Cecilio was lost? And how—in heaven's name—had he known how and where to lead Cecilio to the right place?

In heaven's name . . . Cecilio smiled as he remembered the warm, safe feeling he had in the man's presence, and he realized just what God had done. He would have an even more glorious story to share with his friends in Los Fresnos when he arrived safely home.

WHAT CAN
THE CHILDREN SEE?

Your children are not your children.
They come through you but not from you.
And though they are with you, yet they belong not to you.
—KAHLIL GIBRAN, *THE PROPHET*

c∞つ

B abies and small children—and the purest of spirits in our world, the mentally challenged—seem able to cross the boundaries between heaven and earth in a way that adults cannot. Who among us has not noticed a baby staring fixedly at an object that we don't see and then breaking into wriggling coos and giggles, as if in recognition? What about imaginary friends, the beings that inhabit preschoolers' lives? Are all of them just pretend? Recently, a child who has Down syndrome spoke happily of the "yellow man" who came to his room at night and played with him. His family was perplexed. They showed him pictures in magazines, hoping to clarify his comments. Eventually, the child saw a drawing of an angel. "The yellow man!" he cried in delight, and the family understood. This boy had no words for "shiny" or "golden," so he chose the closest description his limited vocabulary could manage.

On another occasion, two young children were riding in a car behind the one driven by their grandparents. Everyone in the second vehicle saw the grandparents' car suddenly skid off the road and tumble down a ravine. Surely both should have lost their lives in the accident. Instead, each walked away with a few scratches. Days later, when the adults told someone of the episode in front of the children, both youngsters were adamant that something had been left out. One of the children said, "You forgot to tell about the big birds that flew over Grandpa's car." The other child agreed: "And those birds went down in that hole with them too!" None of the adults had observed anything out of the ordinary.

Small children also exhibit uncanny awareness now and then about things the adults in their lives have not taught them. Sometimes this knowledge can be painful, at least at first. Kathleen Treanor knows this well. One afternoon on the way to soccer practice, her four-year-old daughter Ashley suddenly posed a question. "Mommy, would you be sad if I died?"

"Oh yes, honey," Kathleen answered, surprised. "It would break my heart. I'd miss you so much."

"But Mommy," the little girl persisted, "I'd be in heaven with Jesus. I'd be an angel."

"I know that, but I wouldn't be able to hug you. Besides, you're already my little angel." Kathleen was becoming a bit nervous. Ashley had never expressed these thoughts before.

Two days later, Ashley and her grandparents died in the bombing of the Alfred P. Murrah Federal Building in Oklahoma City. The adults had an appointment at the Social Security office there and had taken Ashley along.

For a long time, Kathleen was unable to get past the horror and grief of the event. It was much later before she began to see that during that conversation in the car, mother and daughter had changed places. Ashley, from a hidden wellspring of spiritual knowledge, had been reassuring Kathleen, bringing her a final gift of comfort. "My daughter had gone to heaven, and no matter how hard I chased her, it wasn't time for me to go. I knew she was [there], and I would see her again—she had told me so."[3]

Not all children's brushes with heaven end in tragedy. The majority seem amazing and awe inspiring. For example, Lynette Coldebella, of Palatine, Illinois, is a busy wife and mother who also runs her own business. When Lynette's eighty-five-year-old grandfather, Grundy Hupp, developed Alzheimer's disease, Lynette made time to help her mother with his care. Grundy had been a gruff, independent type, preferring life in a rural cabin in Lincoln, Illinois, to life in the Chicago area. He and Lynette had always been close. "When I was a child, I would go and stay with him almost every weekend," Lynette says. "I loved to listen to his stories of the old days." Grundy was delighted when Lynette's three daughters, Larisa, Tina, and Angelina, came along.

It pained Lynette to see her grandfather deteriorating. He gave up the cabin and moved into Lynette's mother's house. Eventually, the women realized that it was time to move Grundy into a nursing home. "We found a wonderful facility in our area, but soon he stopped speaking." Grundy faded into a coma, and it was difficult to know whether he sensed their presence anymore. During Grundy's final days, Lynette and her mother took shifts so that someone would be with him at all times. Relatives from out of town came and went. Everyone knew they were saying good-bye to Grundy.

One October evening, Lynette arrived at the nursing home at about eleven o'clock at night. Her grandfather lay with his eyes closed, as always, so she sat on a chair at his bedside and became engrossed in the book she had brought along to help pass the time. At around midnight, a nurse came in to check an IV. Suddenly, Grundy's eyes flew open, and he looked directly at Lynette. "I have to go now," he told her, almost urgently. "I have to be someone's guardian angel!" Lynette was astonished. Her grandfather seemed completely lucid, just as he had been before the onset of his illness. Before she could respond, he squeezed her hand—and died.

The nurse witnessed it all. "Sometimes, at the very end, they seem to be looking into heaven," she told Lynette. "But I never heard anyone say *that*."

It was an odd comment. People do not turn into angels when they die, although Scripture says we will become *like* angels, which no doubt refers to our new lives as spirit beings. Instead, souls entering heaven are called *saints* or *members of the elect*. But Lynette did not know anything about angels and had never discussed them or even thought about them. She was sure that her grandfather, who was a good man but not at all religious or church-going, didn't know anything about angels either. Why would this strange remark be on his lips as he left life? Lynette did not have time to ponder. Things had to be done now, people notified, arrangements made, and all while she was grieving. She would think about it later.

The next morning, Lynette's husband, Mark, talked her into attending her bowling team's championship competition. The funeral was being delayed until out-of-towners could arrive, and there was nothing she could do until then. The outing would do her good. Lynette agreed and phoned her younger sister to come by and baby-sit. "Some relatives, along with my older daughter, Larissa, were in the dining room, the phone was ringing, and I was blow-drying my hair." In the confusion in her large three-story house, Lynette realized she had lost track of Angelina, her three-year-old.

Angie was probably playing in her bedroom, but Lynette went to check anyway.

Suddenly, Lynette heard screams from the dining room below. "Angelina! Oh, no!"

"Mommy, Mommy!" Larissa was running up the stairs. "Angie just fell out of her bedroom window!"

"My God!" Lynette and Mark tore out of their room and down the stairs. "I saw some purple fly by the dining room window, Mommy!" Larissa was crying. In a moment of frenzy, Lynette thought, Angie was wearing red and blue, and that makes purple. Lynette couldn't bring herself to go out the door to the stone patio below Angie's bedroom; she was too terrified of what she would find. Instead, as Mark sped by, she grabbed the phone and dialed 411. "It was a mistake, but the information operator sent the paramedics anyway. I kept screaming for people not to pick Angie up, and then I ran and put a blanket over her so she wouldn't go into shock."

Angie was lying very still, but as rescue vehicles screeched into the driveway, she began to cough. Paramedics bundled her onto a stretcher, and Lynette jumped into the ambulance. Mark would follow in his car, but he already sensed that the prognosis was grim. He had seen one of the paramedics look up at the broken screen dangling some thirty-five feet above, gaze at the unconscious child, and simply shake his head.

In the ambulance, Angie tried to speak, but her words were garbled. By the time the ambulance arrived at Northwest Community Hospital in nearby Arlington Heights, at least eight physicians had been notified and were assembling. Angie would have massive internal injuries, they assumed, because she had fallen on the rocks and gravel being used to rebuild the patio. They also expected her to have head and spinal trauma and various broken bones, depending on how she had landed. Grimly, the doctors began their examinations. "They told us that they didn't know how long she would be conscious, so they let both of us stay with her—which was unusual."

Lynette watched the emergency-room scene in disbelief. First Grandpa, now Angie. It seemed too much to bear. How could such a thing have happened? Who would have expected a sturdy window screen to suddenly give way? "I was terrified that Angie was going to die. I cried—but I also tried to pay attention to what the doctors were doing." There would be plenty of time to weep later. As she watched, she noticed that Angie was again mumbling, trying to say something.

"Wings," the three-year-old murmured. "Pretty wings . . ." A few moments later, she seemed to notice one of the physicians. "Where are the wings?" she asked.

The physicians seemed nonchalant at the question—as if they heard it often—but one of them looked up and told Lynette and

Mark to step out of the room. (Doctors have discovered that sometimes children talk more freely about what happened to them if parents are not in the room.) Eventually, a physician came out and approached them. "Are you sure she hit stones? Because there should be gravel embedded in her skin and scrapes in different places. But she has no marks on her."

Lynette was astonished. "No marks?"

"Nothing but some redness on her upper arms. I'm not sure what that's from."

"You mean she's going to be okay?" It didn't make sense.

"Now don't get your hopes up yet. . . ." The doctor was being cautious, but Lynette hurried back into the examining room. It was true! Angie looked remarkably healthy and alert.

"Angie, did you hit your head on the ground?"

"No," Angie answered. "I fell out the screen, and I saw Papa Hupp, and he said it wasn't time. He had beautiful wings, Mommy."

Wasn't time? What was Angie talking about? Lynette persisted. "But did you fall on the patio?"

"No," the three-year-old said again. "Papa Hupp caught me. On my arms. See?"

She lifted her little arms, and Lynette looked. There were no bruises—no scrapes, cuts, or embedded gravel anywhere. Just a few red marks above her elbows, exactly where a rescuer might grab a falling child. "I have to be someone's guardian angel," her grand-father had said. His assignment had been real.

Angie stayed in the hospital for three days as every inch of her was tested and found to be perfectly normal. (She would arrive home on Halloween, go trick-or-treating dressed as an angel, and amaze all the neighbors who had watched and prayed as the ambulance pulled out of the driveway.) The doctors' consensus was that she sustained no injuries from her fall. How this could have happened was left unsaid. Saints and scientists do not often meet. However, as Lynette prepared to take Angie home, one of the emergency-room physicians came to the room and asked to speak with her. It wasn't medical advice that he wanted to share. "I suggest that when you get home, you put Angie back in her bedroom and watch to see if she tries to get out the window again."

Lynette was shocked. She had been planning to move Angie into another bedroom, far from the memories of that window. "Why should we do that, doctor?"

"When little children see angels, sometimes they want to repeat the experience. They're too young to know that it might be dangerous."

"So you think she might deliberately . . . ?"

"Just see if she's afraid of going near the window. That will be a good sign."

Angie *was* afraid of the window, and because of all the safety precautions the Coldbellas took, she never again put herself in danger. However, for the next few years, she often drew pictures of a figure with silvery wings. "It was a beautiful angel, Mom, but he had the old Papa Hupp face on him!" Now, as with many childhood experiences, her memories are fading.

Lynette sees a miracle each time she looks at her daughter. "I never used to believe in angels, but now I do. I don't think a three-year-old would have been so preoccupied with them after falling out a window unless it was true." How it all happened is something she will leave to God. And to one of God's special helpers, Grandpa Hupp.

THIS LITTLE
LIGHT OF MINE

The footprints of an angel are love. And where there is love,
miraculous things can happen.

—*ANGELS IN THE OUTFIELD*, MOVIE

᠆᠊᠊᠊᠊᠊᠊᠊᠊᠊

R obin Lee Shope had never asked God to send her to a mission field to serve him. In fact, she enjoyed being a wife and
the mother of two young children. But when she drove each day
to her job at a school in Lewisville, Texas, it was difficult to imagine a more complex assignment from heaven. Robin taught remedial reading to teenagers who, because of their behavioral
difficulties, were still in junior high school. Many were gang members, lived in single-parent families, or struggled with learning dis-
abilities. Failure, anger, and lack of confidence and self-discipline

were their constant emotional companions. Why should they try? Who cared about them?

Robin was deeply concerned about them. Each day she laid her hands on her class list and prayed for each student by name, asking God to give her the wisdom to address their many needs. She asked the students' guardian angels to help her—somehow—reach them. She even maintained a "rewards" box, so she could publicly praise teenagers who had made a genuine effort that week. But it was an uphill climb.

"Tony was the hardest to handle. He was a Hispanic gang member with a bad temper, sixteen, and still in the eighth grade." The others usually took their cues from Tony. When he was in a cooperative mood, Robin's day was manageable. When he was aggressive or refused to obey, the entire class floundered; they threw items or collectively refused to complete an assignment.

Robin's instincts told her that there was more to Tony than the callous exterior he presented. If only she could break through that shell and bring him the respite and encouragement he so needed. She sensed that he had much to offer the world if he could only believe in himself. "I know you can do better than this, Tony," she would say during their private talks. "Show me some effort so I can reward you." Tony usually shrugged; school was obviously not a priority for him.

One Friday, Robin realized that Tony's behavior had been surprisingly decent all day. Eager to reward him, she announced that Tony could choose something from the rewards box. He ambled up the aisle and took his time perusing the box as if he were selecting a rare gem. Several of the kids snickered. Finally, Tony chose a small American flag. He strutted back to his seat and began to wave it. "Tony, please stop that," Robin asked. "You're disturbing the others."

But Tony continued to swing the flag back and forth as his classmates watched. *Look at me,* he seemed to be saying, and his eyes were fixed on Robin, daring her to do something about his behavior.

He was getting out of control, she knew, headed for a showdown with her. Robin had no idea what to do. Was he capable of physical violence toward her? What if she lost her temper? She prayed silently, asking God to send his angels to comfort and calm the "least of these," the children that no one seemed to want. She looked at Tony, and he glared back. The entire room seemed to hold its breath.

Suddenly, surprised at herself, Robin smiled, breaking the tension. "Tony, if you don't put that flag down, I'll have to sing to you. And believe me, you won't want that!" *Where had that idea come from?* She had only an average voice and had never sung in a classroom before.

But her effort at distraction had failed. Tony continued to wave the flag, a little smile playing at his lips. *Go on, sing,* he seemed to say, mocking her.

Robin gulped. *A deal is a deal.* In a shaky voice, she began a song from church: "Joy is the flag flown high from the castle of my heart. . . ."

The students quieted, seemingly mesmerized. Tony laid his flag on the desk; his dark eyes watched Robin as she sang. Was he angry? "And the King is in residence there. . . ." The last notes died away.

The class was silent. "I haven't heard that since I was a kid in Sunday school," Tony said. "Do you know any more songs?"

"Uh . . ." Robin was astonished at his reaction. He seemed completely sincere, even a little vulnerable.

"How about 'This Little Light of Mine'?" another boy suggested. "We used to sing that at my church."

"Oh, I loved that one," a girl enthused.

Her students had attended Sunday schools, churches? She didn't even have time to ask, for a teenager in the back of the room had already started the next song.

Together, in this most public of school environments, everyone sang one hymn after another; they were reminders of a younger, more innocent time in their lives when they had been filled with hope. "Jesus loves me, this I know. . . ." Robin looked at their faces, heard the sweet purity of their voices, and blinked back tears. Whatever their hardships, they were as beautiful to her as any choir of angels.

After that day, the classroom climate changed. If everyone behaved, then "Sunday school singing" would take place at the end of the day. Robin took requests, connected certain songs to lessons, and exulted at the enthusiasm her teenagers now showed. She gave thanks to the unknown pastors and Sunday school teachers who had planted these seeds in her students. Often she caught Tony's eye during a special phrase and saw that the meaning had touched him too. No one from the principal's office ever reminded Robin that what she was doing was technically against the law.

Tony and some of the others graduated at the end of that year, and Robin lost touch with them. Occasionally, she wondered about Tony. Had those daily moments of relaxation and spiritual peace had an influence on him, enough to keep him from falling back into the ruthless street culture? She would probably never know.

God had other plans. Ten years passed, and Robin continued to teach remedial students. One day she pulled into a car-repair shop to have some work done. The manager of the shop, a handsome young man, greeted her and took her information. He seemed vaguely familiar, but Robin couldn't place him. She was struck by his good manners, but mainly by the sparkle and joy in his eyes.

As he finished the paperwork, the man looked at her. "You don't remember me, do you?"

Robin hesitated.

He smiled. "I'm Tony."

"Tony!" She could hardly believe it. "But how—"

"God reached me through those songs we sang," Tony told her. "I wanted my life to mean something. So I went to mechanics school, and I go to church every week now, and"—he looked around proudly, then back at Robin—"don't give up on kids like me. Keep praying!"

Keep praying. Once again he had reduced her to tears, but now the story was complete. Who had whispered a suggestion of holy song into her ear that day so long ago? Was it her angel? Was it Tony's angel? It didn't matter. A seed planted in the most arid of soils could grow, if it had just a little love and faith to nourish it. She knew that now for sure.

UNSEEN HANDS

Sometimes I hear a flutter
In the middle of the night,
And I know another angel
Just rose up in flight.
—PATRICIA OSBORN ORTON, "THE SOUND OF ANGELS"

K hristy Wallace, a thirteen-year-old from Hugo, Oklahoma, grew up in a warm, spiritual household. Both her grandfathers were ministers, so the extended family all knew about angels. Khristy's widowed mom made sure her children understood that these heavenly guardians were *real*. "Mom would tell us stories about angels and about things that happened that were more than coincidences."

Khristy's mom loved perfume, talcum, lotion, and other fragrant treats. "Every night before she went to bed, she would sprinkle her sheets with a little perfumed powder," Khristy recalls.

Always wanting to be just like her mom, Khristy had also tried this a few times. She had her own container of powder in her room.

One night Khristy's older brother stayed overnight at a friend's house, her younger brother Korey camped out in front of the living-room television, and her mom turned in early. It was a situation Khristy loved—staying up late in her room with the door shut, listening to music or writing, doing whatever she wanted to do, with no one bothering her!

Khristy had a happy night, and at about one o'clock in the morning she decided to go to bed. She knelt and said her night prayers and then decided to sprinkle some of her perfumed powder across her sheets. "I grabbed a handful and tossed it, then turned out the light."

Sometime later, Khristy awakened. She was lying facedown—choking. "It felt like my lungs were bursting because I couldn't get any air." Was this a terrible dream? No, the room was pitch dark, and although Khristy tried to call her mother, she could only gasp. "I couldn't seem to get up either," she explains. In horror, she realized that she had sprinkled far too much talcum across her bed and had inhaled the excess while she slept. Now she was suffocating. "Lord, help me!" was all she could murmur.

Suddenly, Khristy's bedroom door flew open, and the light came on. She heard no footsteps, but someone whacked her back just once. The blow was hard, but air instantly filled her lungs. She could breathe again! Slowly, Kristy rolled over, expecting to see her brother Korey. But there was no one in her room. The entire house was as quiet as it had been all night.

Shaken and still breathing hard, Khristy stumbled out of bed, went in and awakened her mom. Khristy's mom was astonished and immediately searched the house. Korey was sound asleep in the recliner alongside the snoring dog and obviously hadn't heard anything. His mother awakened him, and the three went back into her bedroom.

"Khristy, tell me again how it happened," her mom said. "Are you sure you weren't dreaming?"

"No!" Khristy was adamant. "I felt this huge hand hit me."

"Just a minute, honey. Turn around." Khristy's mom lifted the back of Khristy's T-shirt. She gasped. "Look over your shoulder at the mirror," she told her daughter.

Khristy did. There on her back was a red mark in the shape of a hand. Although starting to fade, it was a definite outline and almost covered the width of her back. The family stared. The hand that had made that print was far larger than any they had ever seen. It could only have come from one place.

Today, Khristy remembers the event as specifically as if it happened last night. "The mark faded, but the memories didn't. I cannot describe how comforting it is to know that God loves us so much that he sends angels whenever we need them."

PROTECTOR
ON THE BRIDGE

Red . . . is the fiercest note . . . the highest light, it is the place
where the walls of this world of ours wear the thinnest,
and something beyond burns through.

—G. K. CHESTERTON

M ax Alley, of Broken Arrow, Oklahoma, is no stranger to angels. As an Assemblies of God evangelist, he has seen their influence on many occasions. During the early years of his ministry, he sometimes caught sight of a man who watched him as he prayed. Unlike the traditional white-garbed being, this man had a fiery red beard and wore a "tomato-soup red" tunic.

"I know it sounds strange, but I'd also catch an occasional glimpse of him, out of the corner of my eye, passing through the house," Max explains. "I had the feeling that if I'd just turned a little quicker, I would have gotten a better view." The "red man" never alarmed Max; he assumed this being was a companion sent from heaven, to encourage him in his work.

Once when Max was in his study fasting and praying for the success of a faltering revival, he caught sight of a huge angel. The angel was dressed in the same red garment, and he ducked under the doorjamb and approached the awestruck Max with a message. Max was not to worry about this revival; God saw, and God would reward him in due time for his effort. Barely a month later, Max spoke at another church, and the event was enormously blessed. The angel's announcement had been true.

Heaven continued to bless Max's mission, and today he keeps to a schedule that would exhaust men decades younger than him. So, early on Sunday morning, May 26, 2002, Max and his wife, Goldie, pulled away from their home and headed for the Assemblies of God church in Arkoma, about ninety minutes away, where he preaches at least once a year. Although an overabundance of rain had swollen the nearby streams and rivers, there was no flooding, and it seemed like any other spring day, bright with promise. Max and Goldie chatted casually as they drove the familiar Muskogee Turnpike and turned onto Interstate 40, the major east-west route through Oklahoma.

They were unaware, however, of an accident about to happen. A huge empty barge was traveling north on the Arkansas River. For no apparent reason, the barge veered slightly off course as it approached the Interstate 40 bridge. Instead of passing under the bridge, the barge slammed into one of its support pillars.

As the barge's six-man crew watched in horror, two long sections of the bridge collapsed into the river—almost in slow motion—at steep angles, forming a V shape. A third section dropped nearly flat, sliding to rest on the embankment. Several vehicles, unable to stop, plunged into the river. "The noise was terrible, and you could feel the ground shake when everything fell," said a shocked witness who was part of a group lining the banks for a fishing tournament. "One tractor-trailer was hanging over the edge. It was unbelievable."

Max and Goldie were completely unprepared. The bridge collapsed just before they arrived at the spot, but, of course, they didn't know it. Max noticed a van ahead of him simply disappear from view. Surprised, he glanced at Goldie. "Boy, I don't remember a hill there!" Just seconds later, the Alleys' pickup truck, traveling seventy-five miles per hour, sailed into the air. Front-heavy, it plunged nose down for about six stories and then crashed into the cement of the third fallen section.

"The air bags went off, and we had our seat belts on," Max recalls. Incredibly, the impact didn't send the engine into the passenger cabin, and the truck didn't flip over or even roll toward the edge, although it stayed in gear. It simply stopped, coming to rest on all four wheels.

Dazed, Max shut off the ignition, turned to Goldie, and saw that her door was jammed shut. Somehow, he dragged her out on his side of the cab. Neither had suffered any wounds; nor did they feel pain—until after they were both on the concrete. Then Max realized he had probably broken his back. He looked around, still dumbfounded.

It was like viewing a scene in an action film. Although no more vehicles had followed the Alleys' truck over the west side, vehicles on the east side were still unaware of the broken bridge. "You could hear the brakes, then see them flying off," says Max. He watched helplessly from below, gripping his truck for support and wincing at the sound of grinding metal, as two eighteen-wheelers and at least four cars went over.

Goldie was praying for her injured husband, for everyone involved. "Can't somebody do something?" she shouted to a bystander as another vehicle fell. "People are dying!" Passenger seats, clothing, chunks of concrete, and other debris floated in the murky water, and several fishermen waded out to reach terrified passengers. Finally, the traffic stopped. Sounds of faraway sirens indicated that, for now, the horror was over.

The Alleys contemplated their next dilemma. How could they get out? Climbing up the steep embankment would be impossible for Max. But as people came down to help them, Max discovered that nothing was impossible, not even walking with a broken back.

"I told the man helping me that the pain was so great, if I wasn't a grown man, I would cry. And he said, 'Well, you go ahead and cry.'" And Max did.

Although rescue teams rushed to the site, only about five people involved in the crashes survived. Many bodies were not recovered until weeks later, when divers were able to move concrete from the river's bottom. Max and Goldie were considered amazingly lucky to have endured the ordeal.

But the couple believes it was far more than luck. "I never touched the brakes on that truck," Max says. "So why didn't it roll into the river?" He believes that an angel of God—perhaps the one wearing a tomato-soup red tunic?—stopped the truck and cushioned them from terrible injuries. "God gets all the glory from me."

Is there a reason that the Alleys survived but others at the scene didn't? Max points out that he "didn't do the choosing" and that God's ways are not ours. But the event has given Max a new respect for eternity. Death often comes quickly, and people shouldn't wait until the last moments of their lives to get to know God. "They might not have time," he says. What a tragedy *that* would be.

KELLY'S ANGEL

They are alive and well somewhere. The smallest sprout
shows there is really no death.

—George Washington Carver

Sometimes it seemed as if that April day in 1999 had happened only yesterday, not twenty months ago, Dee Fleming mused as she sat now in her car, waiting for her husband in front of Columbine High School in Littleton, Colorado. She vividly recalled her husband's phone call, which had propelled her from her office to search for her sixteen-year-old daughter at this very spot. Don had kept vigil at home, waiting for a phone call that would end their terror, while Dee eventually wound up at a nearby grade school with other frantic parents, searching the shocked faces of the students who had fled there. Where was Kelly? Was she, mercifully, out of harm's way, perhaps hiding in a secure place or running with a group of friends to nearby shelter? Would this unbelievable nightmare never end?

The news for the Fleming family would be almost incomprehensible. "One teacher and twelve students, including our Kelly, did not come out," Dee says. Most were killed in the school library, crouching under tables, and their bodies remained there for a day and a half while investigators tried to make sense of the tragedy. The entire world seemed to watch, stunned, as the unfathomable facts emerged. Two student gunmen had succumbed to evil, massacring several people and injuring many more.

Kelly had started her freshman year at Columbine in 1997, shortly after the Flemings moved from Phoenix to Littleton. She had always been shy, and making friends was hard for her at first. But her classmates were soon drawn to her sense of humor, her quiet nature, and her loyalty—when Kelly made a friend, her mom says, it was a friend forever. "Kelly was such a gentle little soul, cheerful and kind. For her to have died amid such hatred and violence is beyond belief."

The Flemings and their older daughter, Erin, grieved in private and took part in the public commemorations and ceremonies. Neighbors and family members wrapped them in consolation and love. Still, life would never be the same. At one point, after examination of the crime scene was complete, the police allowed families to visit the library. Dee needed to say a prayer there and to touch the ground where her daughter's body had lain. "Doing this did give me some relief," Dee says, "but the feeling in that place was oppressive." Dee hurried out of the room. *God,* she asked from the depths of her suffering, *will it always be like this?*

Dee did find one resource that helped stem the pain. "From the time she was tiny, Kelly and I had shared a special interest in angels. Kelly had learned to say the Guardian Angel prayer from a little card her grandmother gave her when she was four." More recently, the two had faithfully watched *Touched by an Angel* on television each week. Dee had begun a collection. After Kelly's death, friends (and complete strangers) sent angel figurines, pictures, and carvings along with condolences. Everywhere she looked, on shelves and tabletops or out in the garden, Dee could see them, reminders of the hope she tried to keep alive. "When I thought of Kelly in that place and how scared she must have been, I wanted so much to believe that an angel was with her there in the library, shielding her from fear and pain on that terrible day."

Christmas 1999 passed in a blur, and the Flemings were unable to rejoice, as were many in Littleton. In the fall of 2000, construction began on the new HOPE (Healing of People Everywhere) Columbine Memorial Library. Originally, the school district had planned to refurbish the existing library, but to the parents of Columbine students, such a plan was inconceivable. They and other community members felt that no children should ever be expected to study in that room again; moreover, they vowed to raise the money needed to remove all traces of the existing library.

The school district bowed to the wishes of the community and began building a new library. The old one, which had been above the cafeteria, would be completely demolished and its floor removed. The space would then be used for a beautiful two-story atrium, with a mural of trees on the ceiling. Fund-raising stretched beyond the Littleton area and across the nation, spearheaded by HOPE. Dee knew that many positive things had come out of this catastrophe, but although she visited the construction site with other families and felt the new life of the school being affirmed, the outer façade of the old library still menaced her. How could she ever heal—even partially—if this memory continued to oppress her?

As December 2000 approached, Dee decided to make her Christmas cards. "I bought an angel stamp and some markers at a crafts store. During my lunch breaks and at night, I stamped and colored the angel over and over again on my Christmas cards." The angel on the stamp was beautiful, with a halo, a long gown, and outstretched arms. In some strange way, the angel brought comfort to Dee and seemed to be helping her through the sadness of this second Christmas without Kelly. Then one afternoon just a week before Christmas, as Dee and Kelly's father, Don, drove home after running errands, Don decided to stop at the school and check the construction progress. "I'll stay in the car," Dee told him. And now, here she was.

She gazed up at the building. She was too close to the area that upset her. It looked the same on the outside as it always had—metal and glass. But Dee remembered the old library space, and sudden tears filled her eyes. *God,* she prayed, *I need to know that Kelly's all right, that she's happy and at peace. Please tell me . . .*

Suddenly she saw it, a white glowing figure moving slowly across the windows of the old library. Not a reflection or a cloud. "I knew instantly that I was looking at an angel. She was elegant, with her flowing gown and halo, and so clear to me." Awestruck, Dee drank in the scene while an overwhelming peace settled around her. In that moment, she knew that her daughter was fine. Angels were with Kelly now, as they always had been.

The burden Dee had carried for so very long was lifting too. Somehow she understood that the old library space, the site of previous malevolence, had been cleansed and healed by the angel's presence, and there was nothing left there for her to fear. She knew that hard times were still ahead, but God had touched her with gentle hands, sending a glimpse of paradise to help her through.

Suddenly, Dee realized that the angel was fading. She fumbled for her camera, opened the car window, and snapped two photos before the figure disintegrated. When Don returned, Dee found herself unable to mention the incident. But she played it over and over in her mind.

In a few days, Dee picked up the photographs. With pounding heart, she flipped through them for the two angel snaps. Had they turned out? Yes, there they were, one an unmistakable image, the second a bit mistier as it disintegrated. . . . and wait! Dee peered at the first photograph again. Why, this angel was familiar. It was the figure she had stamped innumerable times on her Christmas cards, the same halo, the gown, the flowing hair and outstretched hands. Seeing an angel had been gift enough, but the same angel she had stamped and colored for the past three weeks? Dee's heart over-flowed. Her healing had begun.

"The angel has become a gift to many," Dee says today. "I love to share her. People see the figure in the photograph, and say 'Oh my!' or smile or cry. She brings hope and healing and builds faith."

No parent ever recovers completely from the loss of a child. But as Dee has experienced, healing can come. With time, with care— and with angels.

ANGELS ON THE BATTLEFIELD

God governs in the affairs of men.
And if a sparrow cannot fall to the ground
without His notice, is it probable that an empire
can rise without His aid?

—Benjamin Franklin

It is logical to assume that angels have been at the scene of every war in history, including the very first, their own battle in heaven. Lucifer was defeated there, but can anyone doubt that evil is still among us? Certainly, if any group is worthy of protection and encouragement, it is military personnel who willingly lay down their lives to defend others.

Angelic happenings are widely reported from those on the battlefields. The Angel of Mons in World War I, for example, was a female figure in a flowing white gown who led an entire English regiment to safety, then disappeared before their bewildered eyes. A World War II fighter pilot, blinded and flying a damaged plane, was guided to a safe landing by a voice he never identified. Angels do not always rescue those involved in war, but we can be sure that our loved ones are never alone.

It was November 27, 1950, and Sergeant Alfred Green, of Bath, Maine, and his regiment were valiantly battling the North Koreans at the Chosin Reservoir. Alfred had spent more than eighteen months fighting in World War II and had decided to make a career for himself in the U.S. Army, but nothing had prepared him for this ongoing battle. The conditions were brutal: temperatures were thirty-five degrees below Fahrenheit, soldiers were suffering from frostbite, and they had outdated equipment and dwindling rations. The soldiers of the Seventh Infantry Division were told to go east, up the side of the mountain behind them, to replace a marines division that was moving west. Wearily, they started the trek.

"There was only one road," Alfred recalls, "and about an hour into the trip it began to snow. The farther up we climbed, the closer we got to the Manchurian border." The men reached the top at about four in the afternoon, but it was impossible to dig in because of the frozen ground. The soldiers in Alfred's gun section prepared their howitzers in firing position as best they could. The cold, exhausted soldiers did not know that China had just entered the conflict. Unfortunately, they were moving directly into harm's way—the North Koreans were behind them and the Chinese were waiting just ahead.

Around four in the morning, Alfred and the others were jolted awake by gunfire and bugles. "Battery A was to the right of us, just below, and they were being attacked by the Chinese," Alfred recalls. Alfred awakened the seven men under his command. They and the others in Battery B joined the fray. "At daybreak, we discovered that we were completely surrounded. We were losing men at a record pace." It was the most terrible situation Alfred had ever encountered.

The fighting continued for two days as the men fought off the Chinese invasion, but casualties were high. Late on the second day of the battle, high command saw the hopelessness of the circumstances and ordered the soldiers to withdraw from the reservoir area. "Twenty-six trucks lined up, all carrying the wounded, but as they broke through road blocks, the Chinese followed. They were shooting and jumping onto the trucks, grabbing guns and clothes." How were the remaining foot soldiers going to get out of here? He considered the options.

There was a mountain wall on one side of the road, which offered no way of escape. High railroad tracks bordered the other side. Beyond those tracks were rice paddies, and the marines company that the infantry regiment had replaced was somewhere beyond the paddies. But how could they climb up and over those tracks without putting themselves directly in the firing line of the Chinese? They seemed blocked at every turn.

It was now about 10 P.M. Alfred had come to the conclusion that he would soon die. He had already been shot twice in the legs and once in the back. He couldn't remember when he had last eaten or drunk, and the unrelenting cold was unbelievable. Far worse than physical suffering, however, were the sights and sounds of war. He would never forget the moans, the weeping, the bloodstained snow wherever he looked. Slowly now, aware that he was probably in shock, Alfred climbed into the back of the truck and collapsed next to a wounded soldier. "I began to pray my last," he says. "My Catholic background had taught me how to pray, and I asked God to please help me and the others." When he had finished, he got out of the truck and resumed guard duty. What should they do?

It was then that, out of the darkness, Alfred noticed a very unusual man walking toward him. "The first odd thing was that he wasn't dressed for the cold. He wasn't wearing a uniform, or even a hat or a jacket." The stranger was young, clean, and unruffled, an unexpected burst of normalcy in this horrific setting. It was almost as if he were out for a serene Sunday stroll. Before Alfred could ask any questions, the stranger approached him. "You can take your men *under* those tracks," he told Alfred, as if he knew what Alfred had been thinking.

"I've lost my men, and there are many of us who are wounded," Alfred protested.

The young man looked around at the dazed, disheveled soldiers. "There's a culvert down there beyond the rice paddies—you can't see it from here," he insisted. "Take them under the tracks, and you'll be safe."

Albert was bewildered. There was no culvert—he and many others had been in this area several times, and they would have known about it. Why would this stranger say such a thing? And yet, there was obviously something different, even otherworldly about him. A lump rose in Alfred's throat. The man put his hand on Alfred's shoulder and looked deeply into his eyes. "Go," he said gently. "God bless you."

God. Hadn't Albert just asked God for help? Alfred blinked. The young man had vanished, as quietly as he'd arrived. "Spread the word," Alfred told the soldier nearest him. "We're going under the tracks."

It was approaching midnight when the survivors ran for their lives under the railroad tracks. Yes! There was the culvert, in a place where no culvert had been—just as the stranger had promised. Amazed, Alfred and the others scrambled through. The journey was a nightmare: they were ill; some were wounded, wet, and frozen; they didn't have a compass or any specific directions. As dawn broke, the entire group reached safety at the marines' camp. Had it been another few hours, Alfred realized, most of them would have succumbed. "How did you get through?" the astonished commander asked. Alfred had no answer. Who discussed angels in the midst of hell?

Four months later, Alfred was released from a Tokyo hospital and attended a ceremony where he was awarded the Silver Star for action against armed enemy, two Purple Hearts, and a commendation from the Korean government. "I'm accepting these awards for my men," he told the assembly. "They were the brave ones." He gave twenty-four years to his country, found a beloved wife, and today enjoys his four children and fifteen grandchildren.

But he has never forgotten the prayer he said at a desperate moment or the answer that came.

After several years in the quagmire that became the Vietnam War, the situation had started to change. Although the South Vietnamese and American troops had fought valiantly to protect the people from the violence of the communist Viet Cong guerilla fighters, as April 1975 approached, it was obvious that they were losing the war. American consulates in several cities had already been evacuated; Viet Cong and North Vietnamese troops were now approaching Saigon, the capital city of South Vietnam. It appeared that they would settle for nothing less than unconditional surrender and would kill as many military and civilians as was necessary to achieve this goal.

During these years, Lich Lee's husband, Duk, had worked for the U.S. Department of Defense as a technician, and part of his job included repairing equipment. Duk earned an American salary, which by Vietnamese standards was a considerable amount of money. The Lee family had lived for several years in Da Nang, in a huge house; they employed a maid for Lich, and they owned a television, a car, and a refrigerator. When the United States began to pull out of Vietnam, Duk lost his job. His family, which now included two young sons and a baby daughter, had moved to Saigon so that Duk could find work. Saigon was a thriving city, much like those in America or Europe. The family moved into an apartment near the air base. Duk worked for a Korean firm and traveled extensively.

Lich had always been apprehensive about the war, but as had others, she learned to accept it and go on with her everyday life, which was a busy one given that she had three preschoolers. But recently the fighting had gotten closer, and those whose lives had been intertwined with the American presence knew that they must leave at all costs. On April 23, Duk went on a business trip to Iran, but not before arranging for his family to leave Saigon and go to Korea. He had the paperwork processed and purchased tickets on a boat bound for Korea. They would surely be safe.

But it was not to be. During the next few days, word spread throughout Saigon that the American embassy was processing exit visas for its citizens. If the Americans were leaving, what would happen to the South Vietnamese people? Throngs of people attempted to obtain visas of their own from the embassy, and others bribed Vietnamese officials. Marines were posted at the entrances to the consulate to keep people without papers away from the building. "A mood of panic and a sense of fear about being left behind developed during that last week," says one observer. "It was a nightmare, with desperate South Vietnamese looking for ways to escape and authorities trying to break up the lines."

Each day brought more dire news. On April 28, Lich heard the rumble of gunfire. She and the children had remained in the apartment, unsure of their next move. But there was only one chance for them now. They must leave their home and work their way through the crowds to an official, a plane, a boat, to some way out. Lich stayed up all night, and at 4 A.M., fighting down panic, she hid money, some jewelry, and family heirlooms on herself and dressed the children. "Where are we going, Mommy?" her oldest son asked, rubbing his eyes.

"To safety," Lich assured him. In her heart, she was not so sure.

When she reached downtown Saigon, despite the early hour, she recalls that "it was a mob scene. People crowded the streets, trying to force their way through the locked American embassy gates." The city was being bombed, and she watched helplessly as American helicopters and buses began evacuations. Did Duk know what was happening? How would they find each other? She looked at her children's trusting and innocent faces. What would become of *them?*

All that day, Lich wandered the streets, carrying her baby Anh, attempting to find help or transportation, and trying to protect her sons from stampedes that would break out without warning. Artillery rounds and rockets hit a nearby air base, just a few miles away. Reports circulated of advancing enemy divisions. Time was running out. That evening, Lich found a space on the teeming street and laid her exhausted children on it. They cried out for food, but Lich had nothing to give them. She would stay awake to keep frantic people from trampling over them. What would she do tomorrow? Lich had been raised in a Buddhist culture and sometimes prayed to her ancestors. But now she felt an inner stir, almost indefinable. She wanted, no, she *needed* to pray but to someone far more powerful than people. But how did one do that?

The next thing Lich experienced was a swift tug on her clothes. Abruptly she opened her eyes. It was still dark, and she had fallen asleep on the street! The children were sleeping, and safe. A Vietnamese man had been tugging on her clothes, bending over her. "I have a taxi," he told her. "Do you want a ride?"

Lich blinked, but the man was still there. A ride! After an entire day of searching for transportation, a cab driver comes to *her?* Out of all these desperate people? But Lich asked no questions. With the sound of rockets even closer, she and the man picked up the children and put them in the cab. Soon the cab pulled up near the harbor, where a ship stood anchored. It was not an American vessel, but at this point Lich knew only that it represented freedom! If she could get on . . . this area seemed as crowded as the streets she had just left. "Good luck!" the cab driver waved and turned away.

"Good luck to you! Thank you!" she bid him as he disappeared into the deep shadows. She would think about his miraculous appearance later.

The boat, Lich now realized, was for military personnel; to keep civilians from boarding, bars with spikes and barbs had been laid all over the beach. Few people were attempting to cross the hazardous barrier, but Lich plunged forward. As she ran, carrying Anh and dragging the boys alongside, their feet were cut, and the boys began to cry. Then, without warning, the boat left the shore! Lich watched in shock as it sailed away.

In despair, she broke down in tears. The sounds of explosions were closer, the people screaming in terror. There was no place left to run. Would she and the children die here? Would Duk ever know what had happened to them?

But at the other end of the waterfront, Lich saw a second boat, still docked. People were fighting one another to board, but somehow she got through the crowd and approached the actual ramp. Lich looked at it, and her heart sank. It was a thin gangplank, with no railings, swaying in the wind, attached high above the water. She couldn't get across. She had been terrified of heights all her life; she wouldn't be able to balance herself while carrying three children. Frantically, Lich looked around and spotted a man standing in the shadows.

"Sir, who can board this boat?" she asked.

"Anyone—if you can get on," he replied.

Impulsively, she pulled money out of her garments and approached him. "Will you get my sons on the boat, sir?" she asked. "If I don't survive, at least they will have a chance. . . ."

He met her eyes. "I will," he answered, and he took hold of each boy.

Lich looked at them, her heart breaking. Would she ever see them again? Would this man take the money, abandon her sons to the approaching gunfire, and simply leave? It was their only chance. Again Lich felt that inner tug. *God, keep them safe,* she whispered in her heart. God. She had heard about him. Was this a prayer? She knew no other. As the man and her sons disappeared into the night, she returned to the swaying gangplank, which was empty for the moment. Clutching little Anh tightly, Lich closed her eyes. *Help me across, God.* Then, her feet torn and bleeding, she stepped down on the thin strip. It swung, and she almost lost her balance. She would not look; she could not. But she was still upright. Slowly she slid one foot out, then another; her eyes were still tightly shut. She continued on and on. . . . Suddenly, her feet touched something solid, and people on the boat reached out to pull them both to safety. Lich opened her tear-filled eyes.

There, in front of her, stood her sons. How had the stranger boarded the boat with them when she had climbed aboard the only possible way? She would never know. And she never saw the man again.

As the day dawned, Saigon was totally cut off from the rest of South Vietnam. Explosions blasted the city and caused an immediate halt to evacuations. Eventually, evacuations resumed, and the war officially ended as communist tanks rolled down the streets and the last American marines left Saigon on helicopters. But by that time the Lee family was sailing toward Singapore, the first of many stops on the way to America. It would be a year before Duk found his family, and many years before the Lees felt completely at home in Texas, their adopted land.

But Lich will never forget the moment when she discovered God and his angels in disguise. All it took was a prayer.[4]

Sergeant Steve Manchester, a U.S. Army military police officer, was there when the Americans crossed from Saudi Arabia into Iraq in Operation Desert Storm. "It was hell on earth. It took four days before the ground war ended, and history was made." But for Steve, the war was far from over. As did most soldiers, he had more time to serve.

Two weeks after the last shots were fired, Steve was on guard duty at a barren traffic-control point in Iraq. It looked like all the other checkpoints in the region; improvised gravel roads cut in and out amid the sand that was everywhere. (The soldiers found their way around mainly by odometer readings and an occasional map.) Steve was bored and missed his wife. They had been married only a short time, and the heavy gold wedding ring still felt strange on his finger. A lone vehicle approached. It was an American vehicle, so he waved it through. The driver was a medic whose name tag read "Matthews"; he looked confused, but he was wearing a wide grin. "Man, am I glad to see you!" he said to Steve. "I lost my convoy in the dust storm that just passed through. I'm supposed to be on Main Supply Route Green."

Steve chuckled. The entire area was his patrol, and he could have driven the Iraqi roads blindfolded. He gave the relieved Matthews directions, watched the vehicle pull away, and returned to the tedium of the desert.

Several trying months passed. The duty was difficult, especially collecting prisoners and trying to save children who accidentally tripped land mines, all in temperatures that were above one hundred degrees. Enormous dung beetles, snakes, scorpions, and other insects slithered into sleeping bags at night, guaranteeing few hours of real rest. Steve thought that the sand was worse: it was as fine as pow- dered sugar; it stuck to sweating bodies like tar to shoe soles; and it was there when they brushed their teeth, showered, and even ate.

One afternoon as coalition forces began moving south, Steve's pla- toon sergeant, Tony Rosini, approached. "Hey, kid, how about giving me a ride into Saudi?" Tony asked. "My knee's been acting up, and I need pain killers. I can use the time away, and from the look of it, so could you." Without waiting for an answer, Tony slid into the passenger side of his vehicle. Steve followed. Anything to break the monotony.

The men made good time, joking and laughing along the dusty road. As he drove, Steve kept an eye on the vast terrain to make sure they were not being followed. "There were still Republican Guard out on the loose, soldiers who came out of hiding during the dark hours." But they saw no one, and soon they were only an hour from safety in Saudi Arabia. Just then, however, the blue sky turned a blinding orange, and winds swept up the sand. A sandstorm! "It rolled in like a wave, picking up tons of sand and carrying it along," Steve says. "Our procedure was to take cover and wait it out." He slowed, squinting to see the trail.

A sharp bang popped from the vehicle's right side. "In super slow motion, the Humvee tipped left, toward the driver side. The windshield cracked at the top, then spidered through the center. The desert seemed to spin, end over end." A heavy field phone smashed into the back of Steve's skull, and he went limp.

"I felt as if I were being submerged into a pool of warm water. The sensation was heavenly, unlike any peace I've ever experienced. I watched as my life played out before me, like a slide show, with one vivid picture after another brought into the light. I was euphoric." Then Steve thought of his wife. They had barely begun their life together, and he had a future waiting. No, he wouldn't die yet, especially not in the desert!

The struggle was brief, and soon he opened his eyes and through a maze of pain looked first at his left hand. His wedding ring was gone. How strange. He was lying on sand, he realized, and he had obviously been thrown from the vehicle. Painfully, he turned and saw the Humvee, almost forty feet away; lying upside down, its engine was still running and leaking fuel oil. Slowly Steve stood and took a few tentative steps. Then he saw Tony.

Tony was hanging upside down within the wreckage, suspended in midair by a seat belt, and he appeared to be unconscious. The vehicle could blow up! Ignoring his injuries, Steve stumbled to the jeep. "Tony, get out!" he yelled. No response. The engine raced faster, and gasoline dribbled across the sand. Instinctively, Steve unbuckled the safety belt, caught Tony, and dragged him out.

Laying him on the sand a safe distance away, Steve took Tony's pulse. It was faint but there. Tony began to babble. Steve was in shock, but as the army had trained him, he treated Tony's symptoms: *Loosen clothing, elevate feet, moisten victim's lips, shield him from the sun.* "Don't worry, Tony, I'll get us out of this one," Steve murmured. "We'll be okay." The empty words drifted off into the desert. Tony mumbled, shivering in the heat. What were they going to do? Steve removed his shirt and covered Tony's upper body with it; he then struggled back to the smashed Humvee. He realized that, because the sand had blinded him, he had hit a boulder, which flipped the Humvee several times and completely crushed the driver's side. That door was lying twenty feet away. Steve's spine tingled. Had he been wearing his safety belt, he would have been crushed by the weight of the vehicle's roof. Instead, he had bounced easily around, finally thrown safely aside. He had been blessed, but now what?

Tony was seriously injured, so traveling on foot was impossible. They were in the middle of nowhere, with the sandstorm still blowing. They had no food and only enough bottled water for a few hours. Although Steve got on the radio and tried again and again, no one answered his pleas for help. "Nobody knew we existed. The guys at base camp didn't expect us back till evening, so there wouldn't be a search started until tomorrow." Fighting off despair, Steve grabbed his rifle, a box of ammunition, and a ragged blanket. Once again he looked around in the sand for his wedding ring, a symbol of all his hope. But it was a pointless search.

Tony had just opened his eyes when Steve returned. "What the hell happened?" he murmured. Steve explained the accident, adding an apology. Tony raised his hands to the sky. "You worry too much, Stevie boy. Just get us out of here."

"No sweat." Steve looked into his boss's frightened eyes and lied. "I radioed for help. The guys should be here in no time."

Tony grinned weakly and closed his eyes again. Steve bent his head and prayed.

Two hours passed. Tony was in and out of consciousness; Steve was in both physical and emotional pain. He feared Tony's death even more than his own, since he had caused the accident. For the first time during the war, he wept.

Suddenly, the desert atmosphere changed. Was that a sound, a call? Steve's head snapped up, and his eyes narrowed against the still-blowing sand. Something was approaching. Was it the enemy? No! "Hey!" he yelled at an American Humvee, a lone soldier at the wheel. Steve could hardly believe it. Was he dreaming? *Don't go away.*

It was no illusion. The Humvee pulled alongside Steve, and the soldier got out and leaned over to put his hand on Steve's shoulder. "Lay down, Sarge, I'm going to take care of you now. We'll get you out of here." With that, he winked. Steve was stunned. He remembered that grin. It was Matthews, the medic he'd directed a few months ago.

"How . . . ?" Steve started.

"Nice to see you again too!" Matthews answered cheerfully. "I've been assigned the scout vehicle. I'm about ten minutes ahead of our convoy. They should be along real quick."

"How did you know we were here?" Steve persisted, still astonished at Matthew's timely arrival. "Did my radio transmission get through?"

"What transmission? We were just passing through here on our way back." *Back to where?* Steve was going to ask. But instead he collapsed gratefully on the sand. It was time to give responsibility to the medic beside him, however miraculous his arrival.

Slipping in and out of awareness, Steve sensed the soldier working on Tony and then turning to him. Matthews quietly strapped Steve to a long board, cut his pants and shoulder holster, splinted his arm, and administered an IV, all with gentle, capable hands. Steve was safe. More important, Tony was safe. Steve could hear the medevac helicopter approaching in the distance. It was a miracle. . . .

And yet, Steve realized that the convoy Sergeant Matthews was supposedly leading had never arrived. And who had alerted the chopper? He might never know. But prayers did get answered, and now the helicopter was whipping the sand as it landed. Four GIs alighted and ran toward them. Lifting Tony's canvas litter, they carried him to the chopper, loaded him in, and returned for Steve.

"Thank you!" Steve yelled to Matthews as the men lifted him. But the high-pitched whir of the chopper was too loud. There was no way Matthews could have heard him.

With another of those amazing grins, the sergeant ran to the helicopter, ducked under the spinning blades, and leaned inside. Grabbing Steve's hand, he pushed something into Steve's palm. Then, with a thumbs-up, he turned away. Steve opened his hand.

There was his gold wedding band, slightly dented but shining brightly, the promise of new life. How . . . ?

But the time for questions was over. The time for rest and healing had begun. *Thank you, Matthews. Thank you, God.* Steve slid the ring onto his finger and laid back as the chopper took to the air.[5]

War. It is with us always, in some corner of the world. But we can recognize hope too, wherever it appears.

On March 19, 2003, the deadline for the Iraq war looming, Jews in Jerusalem celebrated Purim, God's great deliverance of his people, as recorded in the Book of Esther. At one point during the feast, a majestic rainbow appeared. Observers report that there had been some rain, but at this point the sun was shining brightly—not the usual conditions for a rainbow. But the rainbow grew brighter, as its right end came down in the Judean desert and its left near the Mount of Olives. "As we watched," an onlooker pointed out, "the colors changed, and the rainbow moved and extended to where the ancient City of David rises to connect with the Mountain of Moriah, the Temple Mount." The rainbow reportedly stayed in place for about thirty minutes, and a fainter one emerged above the first arc.

At that same time, Lent was beginning, and the Presbyterian chaplain Major Barb Sherer was looking for ashes to distribute to the

Protestant soldiers in Camp Udairi in Iraq. "Traditionally, we burn palms the previous Palm Sunday and use those ashes the following year as a sign of penitence," Barb says. "But, of course, there were no ashes in the desert."

Not from palms. But there had been a fire the previous week in the central dining facility, which spread to five tents. Amazingly, everyone had escaped, and what could have been a tragedy was regarded by most as a miracle. What better ashes to use, Barb thought, than those left from this fire?

The site was under guard, so Barb brought a cup and explained her request to the officer in charge. Taking her cup, he sent a soldier to the rubble to scoop up some ash. "This enough?" he asked, returning the cup to her.

"Perfect," Barb answered. She put the cup in a plastic bag and went back to her tent. Some of the particles were lumpy, she noticed, so she decided to crunch the ash into smaller fragments. As she dug, her plastic knife hit something metallic. Barb pulled it out. It was a flat metal cross that was smudged from the fire; it bore the memorable words "Jesus is Lord."

Angels, rainbows, new life from ashes—they are all signs to the hungry heart. "The message to me is clear," Barb says. "God walks with us through the terrible firestorms of our lives, and we are lifted unharmed out of the ashes."

THE MAN IN WHITE

If we could be as little children are, we would probably see angels all the time too.
—TERESA KROGER JOHNSON, DeQUINCY, LOUISIANA.

Wars create hardships not only for members of the military but for those left behind as well. During World War II, Americans endured food rationing, shortages of necessary products, and a lack of medical care. Many wives of servicemen, especially those who were expecting babies, moved in with their parents so they would not be alone when their delivery time came, especially in case a physician was unavailable. Mona West Barnes was one of these women. During the time her husband, Harold, was in the navy, Mona and their two little boys, four-year-old Harold Jr. (nicknamed Tootie) and two-year-old Larry, lived with Mona's parents on their ranch in Placerville, California. It made for a crowded household, since Mona's younger brother, Everett, and sister, Vesta, were still at home too. But Mona's mother and Vesta helped Mona care for the toddlers, which was a great help.

Harold had returned from the war, and now the couple awaited the birth of a new baby. Although Harold had a job at the local sawmill, housing was almost impossible to find, so Mona and Harold had decided to wait until after the baby was born to look for a place of their own. The closest hospital was more than fifty miles away, so Mona and her doctor prepared for a home birth. Mona's physician, Dr. Jean, had delivered Larry and was one of the few who made house calls.

One stormy afternoon, after she returned from a doctor's appointment, Mona's labor began in earnest. Her mother called Dr. Jean's office several times, but the doctor did not return the calls. (Later, the Wests discovered that Dr. Jean never received the messages.) With a cold and miserable rain pouring down and concern mounting, Harold and Everett left for Dr. Jean's office. Shortly thereafter, the electricity went out. "This was pretty common during storms," Mona says. "Our ranch was the farthest point from the electric cables, so it usually went out here first." Her father got busy lighting candles, and her mother fed the little boys and got them ready for bed.

Despite the upsets in their lives this past year, Tootie and Larry had adjusted well. However, much of their security probably depended on their routines being the same from day to day. Mona's nightly ritual was to put them to bed, tell them a story, bring them a final drink of water, and hear their prayers. That night, however, Mona's mother took over, since Mona was otherwise occupied. The boys were not happy about that. "I love you," Mona called from her bedroom next door to theirs.

"Mommy, come!" Both boys seemed upset.

Mona believed that one didn't explain labor pains to toddlers. "I can't, sweethearts. Go to sleep."

Eventually they settled. But at about two o'clock in the morning the storm intensified. Harold and Everett had not come home, and the pounding thunder and the lightning flashes awakened the boys again. They were terrified. "Mommy, Mommy!" they cried.

During storms, Mona would go to soothe them and sing a lullaby. Now she was in hard labor. "God, don't let them be afraid," she prayed through the pains. "Let someone comfort them."

But the boys fretted and fussed and kept calling to her. They asked for water. When nobody answered, both began crying very hard. Mona felt like weeping too. Her babies needed her. She wanted to go and comfort them and bring glasses of water to them, but she couldn't. Her father was tending fires in the woodstove and the fireplace and lighting candles and the kerosene lamp. Her mother was getting things ready for Dr. Jean. (Would she ever come? Where were Harold and Everett?) Mona asked her twelve-year-old sister for help. "Vesta, go take the boys some water, please. See if you can calm them down."

Vesta was happy to help. A few moments after she left Mona's side, the boys stopped crying.

Thank you, God, they must be asleep. The entire house seemed to be hushed now. Moments passed. Then Vesta came back into the bedroom. She wore an awestruck expression, and she seemed almost glowing in the dim, candlelit bedroom. How odd. "Are the boys okay?" Mona asked.

"They had water already," Vesta told her.

"How? Who gave it to them? Mom?"

"Mom's in the kitchen. They said the man in white gave it to them."

"But . . ." Mona panted through the next pain, and then argued. "Vesta, you know no one has driven up our hill—we'd know if we had company. What are you talking about?"

Vesta stuck to her story. "All I know is they said the man in white gave them a drink, and they were staring over my shoulder like they could see someone. I looked around, but I couldn't see anyone. But Mona, the room! It was bright and kind of shiny!"

Mona was uneasy. The family never locked their doors. What if a prowler had gotten in and was now hiding in her sons' room? As Vesta went to the kitchen to heat water, Mona's father finished the fires and lamps and came to sit with Mona. "Dad," she whispered between pains. "Please go check on the boys."

"Mona, they're fine. I can't hear a peep."

"Dad, please! Just do it."

A father didn't argue with a daughter about to give birth. When he returned, he wore a dazed look—and a glow very much like Vesta's.

"Dad, are they all right?" Mona asked.

"Yes, I guess so."

"Did you give them a drink of water?"

"They didn't need it."

"But, Dad, they asked for water."

"I'm telling you, they didn't need it!" Her father was obviously disturbed.

"Dad, what happened?"

Mona's father swallowed several times. "When I went into their bedroom," he said slowly, "it was lit up brighter than any light bulb. But Mona, there's no electricity on in the house."

"The room was lit up?" Mona glanced around at her own darkened surroundings. Again, she seemed to sense a holy hush.

"Yes. It was so bright! Then I noticed that the boys had an enthralled look on their faces, and they were staring at the other door. They each had a glass of water in their hands. I asked Tootie where they had gotten the water." He paused and again swallowed.

"Yes?"

"And Tootie said, 'The man in white gave it to us. He told us to stop crying, 'cause it was upsetting Mama, and she needed all her strength. The man in white said to be real quiet and go back to sleep, and in the morning we would have a baby sister, and we could see our Mama.'"

Mona and her father looked at each other. Slowly, they were beginning to understand. Had she not asked for comfort, not for herself but for her little ones, at the very beginning of this night? Had she not asked that someone take care of their needs as well as hers? Why should she be surprised when heaven said yes?

Harold, Everett, and Dr. Jean did not arrive on time; the car had gone off the road into a ditch in those curving, mountainous roads, and after freeing it, the men had gotten lost. So as dawn arrived, Mona's mother delivered her new grandchild. And a few hours later, just as the man in white had promised, the two little boys saw their mother and met their baby sister for the first time.

Ultimately, Mona's marriage failed, and for many years she was a single mother. Numerous difficulties awaited her before she began to reap the rewards of her spiritual faith. But when life seemed grim, she would often remember that stormy night, when an angel came to show her she would never be alone.

ANGELS ALONG THE WAY

Wherever you go, you take your angel. So before you go to any place,
ask yourself whether it's a place that's fitting for an angel to go.

—PETER KREEFT

❦

Sharon Richardson of Kemp, Texas, is a busy wife and mother of four. She has always believed that each of us has our own guardian angel. Several summers ago, she taught at a vacation Bible school. It was the first time in years that such an event had been offered in the Kemp area, and more than eighty children attended, including many from troubled homes. "Not life-threatening situations but homes that were cold or uncaring," Sharon explains. "It bothered me that some of these kids were not being loved in the ways they needed to be."

It was a happy, fulfilling week, and as it ended, Sharon was asked to say the closing prayer. The children formed a circle and held hands. Teachers stood behind them, also holding hands, or attempting to, because there were not enough adults to surround all the children. "I don't even remember what I was praying," Sharon says, "but when I got to, 'And, Lord, we thank you for giving us the opportunity to work with these children, we ask you to give your angels charge over them, protecting them from any harm,' that was all I could say! My mouth froze, because what I saw in the Spirit with my eyes closed just blew me away!"

Sharon was experiencing a vision. "There were huge angels, at least two to three feet taller than us adults, standing wing to wing all around us. At least eight of them, standing in the gaps between the teachers, where the circle couldn't close." The white-clad beings overshadowed the circle, somehow wrapping everyone in an amazing kind of radiance. It was as if God was reassuring her that he indeed kept watch over these little ones, protecting them when no one else could or would. Sharon was overcome, unable to tell anyone about what she saw or even to continue with her prayer. Another teacher stepped in, while Sharon blinked back tears.

It was months later before Sharon felt able to share her experience with the other teachers. When she did, one of them, Patsy, had something to add. "Patsy said that she had felt the presence of angels all that week in Bible class and was especially touched that the 'troubled children' behaved so well. Patsy thought they were probably also sensing angels around them." This was the confirmation that Sharon had needed. God had answered her prayer for the children before she had even finished asking.

She was still thinking about this blessing, when she and her husband later purchased a van. "It was great having something so big and comfortable for the kids and their friends. Especially since we drive a lot." Of course, she put angels in charge of the van.

On a late summer day, Sharon loaded the kids and her mother into the van for the forty-five-mile trip to a Dallas mall to shop for school clothes. "On the way out of Kemp, I noticed that the right front tire seemed low. We stopped by a tire shop, and instead of fixing it, the man recommended that we replace it with a reconditioned tire."

The work didn't take long, and soon they were back on the road. Everyone enjoyed shopping in Dallas and dragged numerous bags back to the van when it was time to start for home.

The weather had been beautiful all day, and Sharon admired the pastoral scene around her as she drove down the highway at sixty-five miles per hour. Midway through the journey, she heard an odd sound, somewhat like a rumble. It sounded as if something was wrong with the new tire. Her eldest, ten-year-old Jonathan, was sitting in the front seat with her.

"Jonathan, can you stick your head out the window and look at that tire?" Sharon asked him. "See if it's wobbling or looks funny."

Jonathan obliged. "It looks OK, Mom, and so does the one on the back." Sharon hung out the window for a moment, looking at the tires on her side. They seemed fine too. Should she stop? David, her toddler, had started to cry, and her mother appeared harried. The other kids were restless. Sharon was uneasy about the noise, but pulling over on this busy road seemed like a bad idea. "Kids," she declared, "it's time to pray." Her children were used to getting this announcement in the course of an ordinary day. Everyone bowed their heads.

"Lord," Sharon prayed aloud, "you promised that you would always be with us and would give your angels charge over us and protect us from any kind of harm. So we're asking you to do this now. Please get us home safely."

"Amen!" the kids chorused.

Ten miles to go, and the rumbling was getting louder. So was little David, who had a stomachache. Over the noise, Sharon and the children now began to thank God. ("As an act of faith, we had to thank him for whatever he was doing.") The miles slid by and finally, enormously relieved, Sharon turned off the highway toward Kemp.

Instantly, she heard a popping sound from the front of the van. She looked at Jonathan. He had been very still on the drive, but now she could see that he was still praying. Sharon turned the steering wheel and again heard the sound, but it was louder this time. Something was definitely wrong with the van.

They could walk home from here. "Kids, we're getting out," Sharon announced. She pulled over, turned off the ignition, got out, and, surrounded by her family, stared at the front of the van.

The replacement tire was barely sitting on the axle. Another foot or two, and it would have rolled completely off. The popping had been the sound of lug nuts flying off the wheel onto the pavement.

Sharon later learned that the mechanic who replaced the tire had forgotten to tighten the lug nuts. He had remembered sometime later and, horrified, had called the Richardson home to warn them. But no one was there. Instead, Sharon had driven sixty-five miles per hour all the way to Dallas and back, with prayer as her only protection.

"Wow!" Jonathan said, still staring at the lopsided tire. "I can't believe we went all that way, and it didn't come off!"

One of the girls laughed. "That must have been one fast-flying angel, holding that tire on all the way to the mall and back!" Sharon's mother shook her head. It was hard to believe.

Today, Sharon occasionally comes across the sign or keychain that warns, "Don't drive faster than your guardian angel can fly!" The saying is meant to be humorous, but Sharon takes it very seriously. "Since this happened to us, we have learned not to take anything for granted. And we ask for divine intervention all the time. God is real—and so are his angels."

HELPING HANDS

We are all visitors to this time, this place.
We are just passing through. Our purpose here
is to observe, to learn, to grow, to love . . .
and then we return home.

—ABORIGINE PROVERB

A s a small boy in Houston, Texas, Rick Bluestein knew angels existed. His mother told him stories of her own experiences and reminded him that everyone has a guardian angel. "Never forget to call upon yours whenever you need some help," she would say.

"I guess I wasn't consciously aware of my angel until I became a Catholic in 1996," Rick says today. "But throughout my life, I've had a variety of beneficial experiences that I now attribute to her." Rick senses his angel as a female most of the time. "She's a pretty good guardian, and she does ordinary things for me all the time, like waking me up for important events, if I might oversleep. Her voice is audible and clear, and always loving."

But this sweet spirit also protects Rick, and he feels her presence quite strongly in dangerous situations. There was the night when he had to make a stop at an automatic teller machine on his way home from work. "Usually I avoid them at two o'clock in the morning, but this time I couldn't." The street was completely deserted, but as Rick waited for his cash, he heard footsteps approaching. He looked up and became tense. Two men and one woman surrounded him, so there would be no way for him to escape. He saw their menacing expressions as he heard the click of the cash being pushed out of the slot. His heart pounded. Having been trained in martial arts, Rick wasn't exactly afraid. But he was outnumbered, and the would-be robbers might have guns. He got ready to defend himself.

Suddenly, all three looked up in unison, their eyes fastened on something behind Rick's shoulder. They appeared shocked, then terrified! Together, they turned and fled, racing to an old Cadillac with no license plates, and screeched away down the street.

Rick was astonished. Had the police stole silently behind him? He turned, ready to thank his rescuers. But the street was as empty as before—at least, to his eyes.

Today Rick and his wife, Ellie, both work at the post office in Albuquerque, New Mexico, and Rick has a side job as an aerial photographer. He believes that his angel got involved when he was taking flying lessons. "I was in the final stages of fulfilling a dream of getting my pilot's license, and one day I was up in a Cessna 150 [a two-seat, dual-control trainer plane] with my instructor, Al Cowling." The men were practicing touch-and-go landings at Houston's Andrau Airport. Andrau has closed, but at that time it was surrounded by cattle ranches as far as the eye could see. Touch-and-go landings involve touching down on the runway and then taking off again without coming to a stop—which helps a fledgling pilot perfect his technique.

The two were in the airport travel pattern, in which all pilots are required to call in by radio the four "legs" of the rectangular pattern used when landing: crosswind, downwind, base, and final. These four signals would alert other aircraft to Rick's position in the traffic pattern.

"We turned on final, to land on runway 36," Rick says, "and I called 'Final!' on the radio, as I was supposed to do. Immediately I heard another pilot also call 'Final!' This meant that another aircraft had failed to use the required rectangle traffic pattern and was flying straight in."

Rick froze. A midair collision was a definite possibility, unless he could break off from his pattern when he saw the other plane. But where was it?

"There are only two blind spots in my Cessna," Rick says, "directly above and directly below." But the plane didn't appear. Rick and Al strained to see, looking every possible way. Nothing there.

Suddenly, Al shouted, "Pull up, pull up *now!*"

Rick had no time to think. He immediately pulled up on the stick, as he had been told to do. Then, incredibly, he saw that Al was pushing in, on his side of the dual controls. What was he *doing?* Confused, Rick released control of the stick to his instructor. But again, right in his ear, he heard the shout: "Pull up, pull up!"

It was almost impossible to pull up against Al. But Rick struggled. "Then I felt a sudden pressure on my hands, something pulling with me." Slowly, inch by inch, the aircraft rose. What the men saw left them breathless. Directly below them, the other plane, a Beechcraft Bonanza, zoomed across their flight path, exactly where they would have been had they not pulled up.

A few moments later, Rick and Al landed safely, shaken but unhurt. After they had settled down a bit, Rick asked Al, "Why did you fight me on those controls?"

Al looked blank. "What do you mean?"

"You yelled at me to pull up, but you were pushing down at the same time."

"What are you talking about? I never said anything to you."

"But—"

"I figured the Beechcraft must be above us, so I tried to go down," Al said. "But I was wrong. Thank God you overpowered me."

Rick has never had another incident in the air. He upgraded his aircraft qualifications recently and not only does aerial photography but also gives aerial sightseeing tours around New Mexico's most scenic spots. Now and then he thinks of those strong but unseen hands that guided him to safety on that very important day. "Thank God," his instructor had said.

Rick always has, and he always will.

PERFECT PAIRS

Miracles . . . seem to me to rest not so much upon faces or voices or healing power coming suddenly near to us from afar off, but upon our perceptions being made finer, so that for a moment our eyes can see and our ears can hear what is there about us always.

—WILLA CATHER

Scripture tells us that when we die, we join that "great cloud of witnesses" that St. Paul spoke about, a community of saints who, like angels, can send little signs of hope to the family members left here on earth, if God wills it. Arles Hendershott Love of Rockford, Illinois, understands this very well.

Arles grew up an only child, but her dad (also an only child) was her best pal, sharing his time and his rich spiritual faith with her. "I was very close to him," Arles says. (Even after Arles married Joe Love, she did not totally change her name. She said it was for professional reasons, but Joe knew it was because his wife didn't want to let go of her dad's name.) Her paternal grandmother, Emma, was also an only child and had been so delighted with Arles's birth that she planted a yellow rosebush in honor of the event. Arles loved her grandmother. "I spent a lot of time with her, and even looked like her. People often called me Little Emma. In her later years, I was her legal guardian and took care of everything for her. When she died, of course I had yellow roses everywhere."

Arles's mother loved to collect antiques and figurines, and her interest rubbed off on Arles. In 1986 Arles started her own collection: Santa Clauses. "I'm not exactly sure how or why it began, but eventually I branched out into other items too." She and Joe enjoyed attending collectors' events and trading with others in the field.

Meanwhile Arles's father had contracted Parkinson's disease. Eventually he needed a wheelchair and a feeding tube, which he handled with great courage and his usual faith. In December 1995, however, he began preparing his loved ones for his death. He asked his wife to buy Arles a specific gift—two Santas for her collection, but not just any Santas. "No, Dad wanted the Santas to be identical, but one big and one little." When she opened the gift on Christmas morning, her dad explained its significance.

"It's to remind you that we will never be apart," her father told Arles. "I'm the big, and you're the little. And even after I move on, I'll be looking out for you and Joe."

"Oh, Dad . . ." Arles's eyes filled with tears. She couldn't think about losing him. But six months later, her father died. The night before his funeral, Arles saw a double rainbow in the sky. One was big, and the other was little.

That should have brought her some comfort. But as the weeks passed, and grief took hold, she wondered whether she would ever be happy again. Life without her father seemed unlivable. Even though she believed in heaven, she found herself wondering: Was he there? Could he see her? Did he know how she felt?

In addition to Santas, Arles collects Egyptian artwork and artifacts. One afternoon she and Joe went to a small store in Milwaukee that sells such things. They bought some papyrus paintings, and the owner rang up the purchase and bagged it. Then he impulsively reached over to a shelf, took an item, and handed it to Arles. "Here," he said. "You need to have this."

It was a brass pyramid. It was identical to one she had at home, only larger. Arles looked at Joe. He was smiling. "Looks like you have a big-little pair now," he said. Just like the Santas her dad had given her, just like the rainbows. It was probably a coincidence. But how had the storekeeper known that this pyramid would have such special meaning for her?

Slowly, more pairs began to come, most through unexplained circumstances. Sometimes the big came first, followed several weeks or months later by the little. For example, two years after her father's death, as Christmas approached, Arles was laid up from surgery, and her mother brought over a Santa for her collection. "I have several hundred now, so keeping them straight can be a challenge," Arles says. "But as soon as I saw it, I realized it was the small version of one I had picked up several years before." Her dad had been with her when she bought it.

Arles also noticed that her pairs seemed to arrive when she most missed her father or was having a difficult day because of her health or her job. Each unexpected treasure brought her much-needed reassurance. One year, Arles joined a Lenox ornament club in which the company sends figurines to members at random intervals. "You never knew when one would arrive," she says. "The day after a particularly rough day, a package came in the mail. It was a big snowman dad holding the hand of a small snowman girl." The timing was perfect. "I took this as a sign that Dad was still watching over us both and that things would work out."

Last summer Arles and Joe came across an exquisite angel figurine holding an armload of pink roses. The angel's name, according to the tag, was Emma. Her grandmother's name! Arles had to buy her. But when she went to the sales associate, she had a surprise. "Emma comes in a smaller version too," the associate explained. "It's the first time the company has ever done that." Arles was getting a funny feeling. Even though the figurines would not be delivered for a while, she decided to purchase both.

The figurines were delayed in shipment. Meanwhile, Arles learned that she would need surgery again. She was extremely worried, so she and Joe decided to enjoy a day in Lake Geneva, a tourist area in southern Wisconsin. "There just happened to be a huge merchant sale going on that day," Arles says, "and everywhere I looked, I saw big-little pairs—carved figures, wood chimes, on vendors' carts, in the VIP area." How she wanted to believe that such a happening was more than coincidence or her imagination, that such little signs were truly meaningful. But could she?

She got her answer a few weeks later, when she learned that her surgery had been successful. That day a deliveryman also brought her a package. Arles had been so absorbed that she had forgotten her Emma angels. Happily she opened the box—and gasped. The figurine she had seen at the display had been holding pink roses. But the roses in both of these angels' arms were yellow—the color that she and her grandmother Emma had always loved best.

Since her dad's death, Arles estimates that she has received some seventy-five big-little pairs. "I believe now that they are definitely messages from my dad, and probably Grandma Emma too. I know they are both safe and with the angels, sending me a little touch of heaven."

MOTHER'S HELPER

The stars are the windows of heaven,
where the angels peek through.

—OLD SAYING

Baby Scott was crying, and Lillian Taylor, of Buffalo Grove, Illinois, stood somewhat dazed beside the stove, warming his night bottle. It had been an exhausting day. "Due to a blizzard and hazardous driving conditions, it had taken me almost three hours to drive home from work after picking Scott up from the sitter," Lillian says. Her husband, Sam, was working a night shift, from 7:00 P.M. to 3:00 A.M., at a new job and had been gone when she finally arrived. Midnight, their huge German shepherd, had greeted her at the door, needing water and a backyard romp. Lillian was enjoying motherhood, but the logistics and physical fatigue were aspects of this new profession that she hadn't gotten used to yet.

The snow was still falling, leaving a thick blanket across the neighborhood. She wondered whether Sam would be able to drive up their unshoveled driveway when he got home. *If* he got home. Forecasters were already calling this storm a major one and warning people to stay at their workplaces overnight. But Lillian would worry about that later. She went into Scott's room, picked him up and changed him, then carried him to their favorite feeding place at the dining-room table. From there, she could see out the living-room window. She was never fearful about being alone. Although Midnight was snoring in his corner, he would be instantly alert, barking loudly if anything out of the ordinary occurred.

Lillian flipped on the large overhead glass fixture and started the baby's feeding. "It was probably only a few minutes later when I heard a tapping at the front of the house." Was it Sam? Lillian looked toward the living-room window and almost leaped out of her chair. There was a woman outside, apparently standing in the hedges! She was tapping on the glass, beckoning at Lillian to come to the window!

"I honestly thought she was a figment of my imagination," Lillian says. "It was almost midnight, and I was so worn out that I just assumed nothing was there. And Midnight hadn't reacted at all."

But a few moments later, Lillian looked up again, and the woman was still motioning. "I'm just seeing things," Lillian told herself. She also noted that the baby seemed to be taking a longer-than-usual time to be fed. She wished he would hurry, so she could lie down, get some sleep, and stop having hallucinations. She sighed. How could she be a good mother with an attitude like that?

She looked up a third time. The woman was still there. In fact, Lillian could see her more distinctly now, and she looked anxious as she continued to motion Lillian forward. For the first time, Lillian realized that this scenario was real. The woman was young, about her age, and appeared to be distressed. Was she lost, or had her car broken down? "I was a little apprehensive, but I couldn't just leave her there without finding out what she needed." Midnight was sitting up now, surveying the window with apparent interest, oddly quiet. He usually barked at anything. What was going on here? Lillian went into the living room and laid Scott in his playpen with his bottle, then turned toward the window.

At that moment, the dining-room ceiling fixture exploded, sending fragments of glass and steel flying throughout the area. The pointed pieces stabbed the chair where she and Scott had been sitting just seconds before and littered the tabletop. Lillian stared at the wreckage, stunned. Just then, she heard her husband's car in the driveway. She ran to the front door and flung it open.

Sam was easing the slipping car to a stop. "They let us go early," he told her. "Why are you out here?"

"There's a young woman at the front window who needs help."

"I didn't see anyone as I drove in." He got out of the car, his boots making deep imprints in the driveway snow. "I'll go over there and take a look." But, as he reported to Lillian a moment later, not only was there no one at the window, there were no footprints in the snow. Only his own.

"But—" The woman had been so real. Wouldn't Sam have seen her if she ran across the lawn? Lillian pulled on her own boots and walked outside for a closer look. She could see Sam's boot prints very plainly, but in the area around the window and hedges there was not a mark in that deep snow.

"My God, what happened to the chandelier?" Sam was regarding the dining room with shock. Lillian went in. There was glass all over, the baby was safe in his playpen, and Midnight was snoozing again contentedly. For the first time, Lillian's knees began to shake. What a close call they had just had! The baby could have been seriously injured, even killed! Glass in his eyes, or hers . . . She looked at the shards and shuddered.

Then, suddenly, Lillian understood. The figure at the window had not been in trouble. She and Scott had! Nor was the lady a flesh-and-blood woman, even though she looked like one—which was probably why Midnight had not barked at her. "My parents had always told us kids that we had at least one angel to protect us," Lillian says, "and I had believed that." Now she realized that either

her or Scott's guardian angel had alerted her to the impending danger and moved them both out of harm's way.

In the midst of that winter night, warmth flooded Lillian. She did not have to worry about being a perfect mother, for she was not the only one watching over Scott. She looked out the window, smiled at the stars, and went to find a broom.

TERRY'S DOLLS

I have found that if you love life, life loves you back.
—ARTHUR RUBINSTEIN

One of the delightful surprises of the angel "renaissance" of the 1990s was the craftspeople and entrepreneurs who unexpectedly benefited. Since an increasing number of people wanted to start collections of angels, or at least hang a picture or two, little shops sprang up, and talented artisans created merchandise for others to buy. (By 1996, more than two hundred angel stores had opened, not including those on the Web.) Some of the creations were a bit over the top, and an occasional customer purchased cherub shower curtains just to be part of a trend. But beneath the surface, it was obvious that people were learning to love angels and the reassurance they brought.

Terry Dorkins was one of these. The daughter of a military man, her family moved often, and she continued the tradition when she married a soldier during the Vietnam War. Terry worked at the

Pentagon and later for NASA. Eventually her family landed in Durham, North Carolina, where she started her own business of creating computer graphics for a corporate clientele. She also developed a serious lung illness, chronic obstructive pulmonary disease, which was complicated by pulmonary hypertension. "I kept going," she points out, "because there really wasn't any other choice." For various reasons, her financial situation was shaky.

By December 1998, her illness had intensified. It became so difficult to move and to breathe that she found it all but impossible to get from the handicapped parking space in front of her office to the front door. "I had to give up my clients. I had always been productive, active—and this was terribly depressing. I have a little office in our home, so I would sit there and pray. What was going to happen with my health? And if I was this sick, how was I going to earn any money?"

As she prepared for Christmas that year, Terry unearthed a porcelain tree-topper angel she had purchased at Wal-Mart several years before. Originally, the angel had worn white satin and had quilted golden wings. Over the years, Terry had added a halo, a locket, and even a little bag holding a "gratitude list" of blessings she had received. "After Christmas that year, instead of packing her away, I moved her to my home office. That's when angels began to take over my life."

One day Terry was at her desk, praying for solutions to her numerous problems. She looked up at the angel on top of the filing cabinet. "She was under the glow of a torchiere lamp, and she looked kind of . . . radiant." She also looked a little worn, as if she too needed some tender loving care. *I should remake her,* Terry thought. At once she realized what a silly thought it was. Despite her accomplishments in other fields, Terry could barely thread a needle. She had never done any sewing, not even hems or button replacements, and had fallen short when trying other crafts. And what did this have to do with her current dilemmas anyway? Shouldn't she be trying to solve them?

Maybe. She decided to spend a little time with the angel first. When she had redesigned the gown and replaced the quilted wings with real feathers, Terry was astonished. "I put her back on the file cabinet, and she was beautiful. I was so pleased. It occurred to me that maybe I could make angels for other people."

Terry found a professional doll maker on the Internet. This woman put Terry in touch with a doll maker in her own area. Both were happy to teach and advise her, especially about working with porcelain. To pay for her lessons and supplies, Terry began selling one-of-a-kind angel tree-toppers to selected friends and family. One day she put up a Web site displaying the dolls, and she traveled around the Internet visiting similar sites. She came across a guest-book entry from a woman named Johanna. "I e-mailed her, invited her to visit my site, and as time passed, we became good Internet friends." This was all interesting, and Terry was feeling a bit stronger emotionally as a result of the encouragement her new Internet friends were providing. But the bills remained, and so did her lung condition. What should she do?

One autumn day in 1999, Johanna e-mailed Terry. Would Terry make a special angel in memory of Johanna's granddaughter, Samantha, who had recently died of a chronic illness? It was a difficult assignment. There was so much emotion involved—and this was Terry's first attempt to please a real customer. She worked as hard as she knew how. The results were exquisite, and Johanna was very pleased. But Terry couldn't get Samantha out of her mind. The little girl had been a patient at Duke University Hospital, just a ten-minute drive from Terry's house. "I thought about how many Christmases she had been in the ICU and I wondered about the other kids there. Would receiving an angel make their Christmases better?"

It was not difficult to find out how many children would spend the holidays in intensive care this year. Terry explained her idea to the hospital's children's coordinator, and the woman immediately asked for thirty dolls. Thirty! Terry hadn't expected that many, but she went home and started sewing. Thirty. Forty. Fifty. . . . She felt compelled to make more. "Just a few days before Christmas, the coordinator phoned and said there were going to be seventy children in the intensive care unit over Christmas. I had made seventy-two dolls, and I brought them all."

As it turned out, there were not seventy small patients in intensive care that year. There were seventy-two. Every child received an angel, even the preemies; each had one tucked over the miniature beds, watching over them in true angel fashion.

All of these dolls had been done at Terry's expense, and money continued to be tight. Terry knew she should find a job that she could do from home. But she *had* a job, didn't she? Although God sometimes seemed very far away, Terry sensed that making angels *was* her calling, at least for now. Slowly, orders started to come.

In addition to selling her angels, Terry continued to make ones to donate to the children at Duke, at least sixty each year. She told very few people about this venture, preferring to remain anonymous and let the angels themselves be the focus. It was an up-and-down time for her. "My lung situation got worse. But I was making friends with almost everyone who ordered from the Web site. Even though I never met them, they became a prayer community for me. Their friendship gave me such strength. I was helped especially by Johanna, who had purchased the very first doll." Every day was a new venture, a gift that she used with enormous gratitude. Oddly, every doll she made seemed more beautiful than the one before it. Who would have thought this "noncreative" person could design and make such items? "I have to believe it was God who put me in the angel business," she says. But God wasn't finished yet.

In January of 2003, Terry learned that she would need a lung transplant. Doctors projected that even with the transplant, she might live only five years at best. And there was another unanticipated problem. "When you prepare to be placed on the transplant list, you are told that you will probably need several blood transfusions during the surgery," Terry says. In many cases, it is the patient's responsibility to provide much of this blood. "But my blood type is unusual, A negative. I contacted everyone in my extended family and learned that there was not one potential donor among them. Only my deceased mother had my type." Because of this, Terry could be dropped from the list.

So close, and yet so very far . . . Terry went back to her home office and gazed at her angel, still atop the filing cabinet. God had brought her through so much since the day she had repaired that little figure. She would not doubt him now. She turned on her computer and told some of her Internet friends, who already knew of the impending surgery, about the blood problem. That evening, Terry received an e-mail. "My daughter and I are both A negative. We'll be glad to donate blood for you." Terry looked at the return address and got goose bumps. It was from Johanna, her first customer, her prayer partner, someone she never would have met had she not started making dolls.

In March of 2003, Terry met with Duke's transplant director. By now her entire e-mail list—and all of their intercessors—was praying for her. As she entered the office, she felt surrounded by love, comfort, and angels, of course. There was a surprise in store: "Some things seem to have changed," the doctor told her. "You do not need a transplant, at least not now. And your heart is quite stable. We think medication will be the best course for you." Terry gasped. Had she been given a healing?

Yes and no. There is no cure for her condition. "But now that I know I'll be sticking around for a while, I can see myself working on my angels, even launching a new line of heirloom angels." She has no time to worry. There is work—and loving—to be done.

One cannot outgive God. Was Terry's generosity to others a cause of her own renewed health? It cannot be known. We can only wish her joy and watch to see what the angels do next.[6]

NICOLE'S SPECIAL SHOES

I saw the tracks of angels in the earth,
The beauty of heaven walking by itself on the world.
—Francesco Petrarch

Bambie and Francis live in Pasay City in the Philippines. Francis is a software developer and a systems analyst for a large information-technology company; Bambie works in a bank. They have a four-year-old daughter, Nicole.

One Sunday evening, as Francis and Bambie were preparing for the Monday-morning rush, Nicole brought her shoe to Francis. "Daddy, see? The buckle doesn't work."

Trust a child to wait until the last moment! Francis examined the shoe. The buckle was indeed broken. "I could not let my daughter go to school with a broken shoe," Francis says, "so I decided to go to the shoe-repair shop right away." He found a pair of Nicole's outgrown shoes with two intact buckles. "To save a little money, I decided to bring those shoes in too, so the repairman could use the old buckles to repair the newer shoes."

It was a small, open neighborhood shop, and Francis had been there several times. There were two benches in front that faced each other. Someone was sitting on one bench, so Francis sat on the other, holding the two pairs of shoes. He was in front of a glass shelf, where shoes were displayed. Despite the darkness falling, the street was busy, with people talking and hurrying along. He began to think of his plans for the upcoming week.

Suddenly, Francis felt himself pushed forward and aside, almost completely off the bench. As he struggled to regain his balance, he heard four loud popping sounds. Gunshots! Shocked, he ducked and, along with some others, ran through the shop and got behind the counter.

"Sounds like someone's being robbed," the shoe repairman said, his eyes wide.

"In this busy area? No way," one customer answered. "Let's go out and look."

"Better not," Francis said. He had a strange otherworldly feeling, and the left side of his body—where he had been pushed— was numb. He knew without a doubt that he and the others should stay where they were. "You can check everything out after it's safe," he told the others firmly, "but not now." The others shrugged. Suddenly, more shots rang out. People looked at Francis. He had been right.

Within minutes the shooting had stopped, and the police arrived. Witnesses began comparing notes, but everyone had been caught off guard, and there was little solid evidence available. Francis learned that the computer shop next door had been robbed, and there had been a shootout between the shop's security guard and the robbers as they ran away. Curious onlookers were gathering at the repair shop's shelves, looking at something on the ground. Francis went over to look too.

What he saw ran a chill up his spine. Two bullets had pierced the glass display shelf that was behind where Francis had sat, and broken glass lay all around. One of these bullets, a .45 caliber, had landed behind the shelf on the ground. The other, a .38 caliber, had also punctured the shelf and was sitting on top of a pair of displayed shoes. Two wild shots, from two different guns, both traveling directly at Francis. "One bullet would have pierced my lung, and the other my spine, if I hadn't moved before the bullets hit."

But he hadn't moved. Someone else had pushed him. Francis stood, remembering the powerful shove and then the numbness along his left side, which had brought him almost to his knees. There was no room for anyone behind him to stand. Could it have been his guardian angel, making sure Francis was out of the line of fire? "I have always believed in guardian angels. But this was the first time that I had ever felt anything physical."

What else could it be? The shoe repairman approached Francis. "If you want to wait, I can repair those shoes now," he said, still a little shaken.

"I can wait," Francis agreed. He knew he had nothing to fear.

When he arrived home and told Bambie what had happened, she was as amazed as he was. "I haven't been very religious," Bambie says. "But there is somebody out there looking out for us. And I thank him very much for his blessing of life and love."

NEARER THE INFINITE

There is an old saying that before a baby is born, God kisses its soul.
And as its guardian angel bears it earthward to its little body, he sings.
Is there, in my subconscious self, still a dim memory of that kiss,
a faint echo of that song?

—PRAYER AT A GREEK CHRISTENING

When Jeanie Taylor was a preschooler, she went through a trauma. She says that during that time, beings of light came to comfort her. "I saw angels, but I'm not sure if I was seeing with my natural eyes or with my spiritual eyes. They did not have any wings, and they seemed to be made of white light, in the form of humans, with substance, not just air." Jeanie does not remember the angels speaking words to her. Instead, they sang beautiful music, which left her feeling completely peaceful, warm, and protected. "I may have been having an out-of-body experience," she says, "but it seemed quite real to me."

The episode was particularly meaningful to Jeanie because she was already interested in music. Her parents had noticed her talent early and would eventually provide lessons for her. She learned to perform and teach flute, piano, guitar, violin and other orchestral strings, and voice! When she was ten and going through another difficult time, the angels returned. They sang indefinable but exquisite music to her, which again helped heal her. "After that, I occasionally heard them singing along when I was singing, usually in choirs for school or church." But she learned early not to speak of this unusual blessing to others, not even to her parents. "I wanted to be accepted as one of the group, and people would think I was hallucinating or making things up."

When she was sixteen, a car Jeanie was riding in rolled over into a lake. Once again the angels were there, "and this time, they caught me in their arms and held me safely," she says. "I received only a few scratches in the accident." Typically, she told no one about her heavenly helpers, but now she began listening for their presence. And, as she married and raised her five children, it came.

"I've heard them singing at funerals, weddings, and other places. Sometimes they sing a cappella, and at other moments they are accompanied by orchestra, organ, or other small combinations of instruments." Jeanie has heard music she recognizes, such as the complete Hallelujah anthem from Beethoven's "The Mount of Olives Oratorio," and simple hymns with additional *amens* added to the endings. She has listened to the work of Bach, Handel, and Hayden, but she has also encountered original themes, sometimes laced with sounds unlike any she's heard on earth. "The strings are sweeter, the winds more mellow. The heavenly musicians are not as limited in range, instrumentation, or style as we seem to be."

Jeanie has carried her own music across the world, teaching and performing in foreign countries and in several states. She writes carols each year and sends them to her friends and family as Christmas cards. "Often, these melodies awaken me in the middle of the night. I have to write them down immediately because they are sometimes gone from my mind by morning."

But the angels come most frequently to Jeanie during ordinary times, "perhaps when I am meditating, or noticing how beautiful something is. In my personal search for peace, I have learned to look inward. And this music of paradise has often served as an answer to prayer for me."

It is also a tender guide. After being single for quite a while, Jeanie began to date in 2002. She and John met at a church singles' dance, and they attended a church concert together the following night.

About halfway through the presentation, John realized that he was hearing an additional choir. The singing filled his spirit, and he realized that—strange as it seemed—the music was somehow celebrating him and Jeanie being together! How could this be? John was so moved that tears ran down his cheeks. Jeanie noticed but kept her composure until the two reached the parking lot. "You won't believe what happened!" John burst out. His story, and the emotion it evoked, was so similar to what Jeanie had often experienced that, risky as it was, she admitted her own experiences. The two knew they had been touched in a miraculous way, and they began to fast and pray for guidance.

"We received the answers we were looking for and were married just a few months later in my daughter's beautiful backyard," Jeanie says. "I thought it was a perfect example of God's sense of humor, since it was John, not me, who heard the angels singing on our first date!"

"Music is well said to be the speech of angels," Thomas Carlyle once remarked, "and it brings us near to the infinite." Jeanie agrees. It has blessed her life profoundly, although she cannot explain why it happens. "I'm not any more righteous or needy than anyone else. This music of the spheres brings me instant bliss, but it is not earned." It is a grace, and she is content to enjoy it when it comes.

DEFEND US IN BATTLE

God has something planned for each of us, and he does protect us.
But after a while, if we keep rebelling against him, our protection runs
out. If we live for him and try to stay in his will, we will be protected
until he wants us to come to live with him in heaven.

—NELL BERRY, STOUTSVILLE, MISSOURI

Louis Saia was born into a large, close-knit Sicilian Italian family in the New Orleans area. "I went to Catholic schools and practiced religion as an obligation until I got out of the house," Louis admits. He finished college, then worked in the family trucking business. Even after marrying and starting a family, he hung out with other tough young men who were not exactly looking for trouble but were never at a loss when it came. In 1986, the Saia family sold their business, and the buyer asked Louis to stay on and run it as president. He did so for six years, then tried to buy the company back. He failed and decided to resign.

Despite his rough exterior, Louis had always been extremely talented and inventive. Now he worked on developing a "pallet reefer," which was actually a new way of shipping refrigerated products. "In my travels I had noticed that there was a huge market for fresh seafood in the South, yet no really practical way to ship it out every day. It took a week to fill a big refrigerated truck with perishables, and by that time, the seafood wasn't fresh anymore." Louis designed a stackable shipping container, cooled by its own compressor, like a refrigerator. It could be filled by a forklift and immediately shipped alongside any other kind of load. He took out four patents on his designs.

Pallet Reefer Company was an instant hit. Louis was soon receiving calls from trucking firms that wanted to order the device. It was time to take in a financial partner, he decided, so he could manufacture his invention on a large-scale basis. A major corporation bought a 50-percent share of Louis's invention and promised to finance its development with $25 million. In 1994, however, a larger firm bought out the corporation, and the executives who had negotiated the original arrangements with Louis were gone. The new company wasn't sure it wanted to be in the trucking business. It would spend time learning what Louis was doing, he was told. Perhaps it would sell its half back to him.

Louis was impatient to get started. "But my staff and I spent the next several months answering all their questions and taking them to visit potential customers. Everyone was enthusiastic. The boss of one trucking firm in California said he would buy one thousand units immediately, if he could." At that day's end, in a trucking parking lot, the executives approached Louis.

"We don't like owning 50 percent," the company representative told Louis. "We'd like to own it all."

Louis was stunned. "I don't think I want to sell," he told them.

"We'll give you $2 million," someone else said.

"But we'll easily earn that this year alone, and we have fifteen years left on my patents," Louis protested.

"You don't get it," the rep replied. "If you don't take the $2 million now, when we're through with you, you'll have nothing. You'll be bankrupt."

The men stared at Louis. It was the age-old game, the powerful against the small. These executives had seen the value of his invention and were simply going to take it. Shocked, he drove out of the parking lot and hopped a plane for New Orleans.

"It's important to understand where I was spiritually, at this point," Louis says. "My ambition wasn't eternal life but to be a rich and powerful businessman. I went to church maybe once or twice a year. If good things happened, it was due to me, not to God. I hung around with a bad crowd and was a deplorable example for my children." Now, perhaps, he would reap what he had sowed, but not without a fight. Instead of accepting the company's offer, Louis and his wife, Cindy, decided to sue for breach of contract.

"The next year was a nightmare," Louis says. "We had litigation in three cities at the same time. I hired lawyers, sold some property, mortgaged my house, borrowed on every asset, and even borrowed from my family." (A patent case that goes to trial can cost more than $500,000, and Louis was involved in several cases at the same time.) He thought he had known what stress was all about, but as things dragged on, he suffered panic attacks that kept him up all night and painful stomach ulcers. "I started to drink to relieve the symptoms and took five or six Valiums every day. But nothing helped. Each night I would pace around the island in our kitchen, so many times that eventually I wore away the stain on the wood floor."

Worse than the worry was the anger. These men were stealing his business, just as they'd promised, harming his family and his workers (who by now were not even drawing salaries). In his worse moments, Louis actually thought about hiring hit men. He had connections, and fighting this kind of evil wouldn't be a sin, would it? Although Louis had been away from God for a long time, his conscience had been formed correctly. He abandoned that idea.

Ultimately, the money ran out, and most of the lawyers resigned. Even Louis's father refused to lend him any more. "Son, you picked the wrong fight," he said. "You have a better chance of winning the lottery than beating the big guys."

Louis and Cindy were down to $60 in their checking account one Sunday morning. "Louis, come with me," she asked.

"Cindy," he said, pointing to the worn wooden trail on the kitchen floor. "See that? I can't sit down for five minutes—how could I last a whole hour in church?" He felt as if he would explode from the inside at any moment, and he was out of Valium. Death would have been welcome. He would go running, he decided. Anything to get out of the house.

Louis ran down the gravel road behind his house as fast as he could, trying to outrun the feelings, the terrible apprehension that now ruled his life. Like a broken record, the anxiety played in his mind. How? Why? What to do? His small office building was at the back of his property, and as he turned toward it, he noticed someone standing on the porch. His secretary? But it was Sunday. Getting a little closer, Louis realized that the woman was not his secretary. She was no one he had ever seen before. She wore an old-fashioned white gown and veil, and a little bit of her light-brown hair blew in the breeze. She had extremely blue eyes.

"I got scared," Louis says. "I was too close, seeing too much, and I knew I wasn't hallucinating." He would run right past her, he decided. But as he approached the porch, he met her eyes and was stopped cold in his tracks. He stared at her. Why was she here?

She seemed to read his mind. "I am praying to protect you," she said quietly. "Just have faith in my son, Jesus."

Louis could hardly believe his ears. In his usual decisive way, he walked right up to her. "When I got close, she looked as human as anyone. Then I went to touch her arm, but there was nothing solid there." It was then that he fell to his knees, praying to God in a way he never had before. In moments he was flooded with joy. He opened his eyes, and the lady was gone. But the bliss remained. "In an instant, I had gone from the worst despair I'd ever encountered to the best moment of my life. I had been dying from stress because of living the wrong way. And she said everything I needed to hear."

Cindy was astonished when she returned from church and found a calm and smiling husband. Some of his family dropped by as well. "What happened to you?" everyone wanted to know.

"I saw the Blessed Mother Mary on the porch this morning," Louis announced.

His family exchanged glances. Obviously the stress had finally caught up with him. Should they bring him to the hospital?

But days passed, and Louis remained joyful. For many years he had not prayed, but now he couldn't stop. Praise broke from his lips at unexpected moments. He was happy to be alive, appreciative of his wife and family, aware of an occasional unexpected scent of roses. The lady's words echoed in his spirit, the only words he had ever needed to know: "Just have faith in my son, Jesus."

What, specifically, did this mean? Amazingly, Louis wasn't concerned about it. He would be guided wherever the Lord wished him to be, at the helm of a company or driving a truck, living in splendor or poverty, it mattered not. His healing had begun. He would wait upon the Lord.

Gradually the answers came. He was to pursue his court cases, and the money to do so would be supplied. Soon new lawyers appeared, willing to take his case on a contingency basis, and a bank vice president decided to lend him $5 million with no collateral. In March 1996, despite their lawyer's advice to stay home, Louis and Cindy went to Delaware. Because of the deadlock between Louis and the corporation that owned half his invention, the corporation had petitioned a Delaware court to liquidate the company that it had formed with Louis. If liquidation happened, it would force the sale of his patent, which the company could then acquire inexpensively. The judge, Louis was told, had already indicated that he would rule for the corporation, and there was no need for Louis's presence. "But the aroma of roses was especially strong that previous week," Louis says, "and I decided to trust it, and go."

In court, Louis prayed calmly, despite the smirking of his opponents. *Lord,* he found himself asking, *please let the judge know that these people are using his court to steal.* The case lasted several days, and it was obvious that Louis was going to lose. Then, the judge delivered his verdict. "What if these people are using my court to steal?" he asked, using the exact words Louis had used. In a stunning surprise, the judge ruled against liquidation. Arbitration was the only way to settle the dispute.

They had won this round! Out of court, Louis could no longer stem the tears. He dropped to his knees on the sidewalk in Rodney Square and wept. Passersby stopped to help, assuming he was ill. But Cindy waved them on. Tears could be joyful as well as sad. And Louis had much to be joyful about.

Just a few weeks later, a priest whom Louis had never met came to visit him. The priest had a strange story. "In a vision, I saw you kneeling on a sidewalk. You were wearing a navy blue suit, white shirt, and a yellow tie." Yes, Louis thought—the exact clothes he had been wearing that amazing day in Delaware.

"Standing in front of you, about nine feel tall with wings about fifteen feet high, was a magnificent angel," the priest said. "I believe it was Michael. His sword was drawn and touching your head. He was doing battle for you. I wanted you to know."

Louis was stunned. "I had never thought of the power of angels, about how they protect us, not only against physical danger, but other kinds of evil." He had one question for the priest. "What day did you have the vision?" he asked.

It was the same day Louis had fallen on his knees in Delaware.

Other cases followed, and Louis was the victor in every one. By the time all litigation had ended, his patents had been restored to him and the corporation owed him $26 million dollars in damages and costs. He was able to pay his lawyers, open a factory to begin production of his pallet reefer, and make large donations to charity. He turned his office into a small chapel—holy ground—and welcomed people who wished to pray there.

Louis also commissioned an artist to paint a picture of the archangel Michael as described by the priest. The picture was reprinted on cards, which Louis carried with him at all times. "I would go up and down the French Quarter, giving cards to the prostitutes and drug addicts who hang out there," he says. "I told Michael I would be his lowliest foot soldier. Whatever he wanted me to do for him, I would."

Soon Louis had built his own trucking firm, and he decided to put the same picture of Michael on the side of his fleet of trucks. Today more than seventy trucks bear the logo of the St. Michael's Express as they crisscross the country, a ministry on wheels. "Prospective drivers see the angel image and they call," Louis says. "The image strikes a chord with drivers who have certain values, and they're the kind we want working for us." Drivers also carry holy cards and are instructed to give them to anyone who asks.

Louis continues to await assignments from the archangel Michael, and he gives thanks each day for what his life has become. "I was certainly happy about the court verdicts," he says, "but nothing comes close to the real victory I experienced—my conversion. And it deepens my appreciation for what faith can do for us, especially in no-hope situations, like a major illness, a child on drugs. There is no such thing as no hope. God can do anything."

So if you happen to be traveling on a super highway and you pass a truck sporting the name St. Michael's Express, give the driver a wave. Like you, he and his boss believe in angels.

BEYOND COINCIDENCE

We should get to know the angels now
if we wish to spend eternity with them.

—POPE PIUS XII

⚜

Research shows that the elderly have mystical experiences almost as frequently as children. How nice to know that, even when we aren't there to care for those special relatives and friends, the angels know what to do.

Paul and Mona Barkley, of Schaumburg, Illinois, had a deep affection for Cardinal Joseph Bernadin. They had been impressed with his humility when he was appointed to lead the archdiocese and introduced himself to Chicagoans as "Joseph, your brother." Years later, when it appeared he was losing his battle with pancreatic cancer, they were inspired by his acceptance of God's will.

When the cardinal died on November 14, 1996, church officials planned a funeral Mass at Holy Name Cathedral, followed by a slow procession through Chicago's North Side and West Side to Mount Carmel Cemetery in Hillside. The Barkleys wanted to pay their respects, but attending the funeral Mass was not an option. Most of the seats would be reserved for dignitaries or "important folks." In addition, Paul has a condition called peripheral neuropathy and needed a cane for walking support (today he uses a wheelchair). But the Barkleys were familiar with Mount Carmel Cemetery because two generations of Paul's family were buried there, including a cousin, Archbishop William D. O'Brien. They decided to watch the Mass on television that day, then drive to Mount Carmel, park somewhere nearby, and watch Cardinal Bernardin's procession pass.

It was a practical plan. "What we didn't count on was how long it would take the procession to arrive," Paul says. Thousands of people flooded the route through the city, and vehicles in the line drove at a crawl. By the time the cortege had reached the cemetery, it was almost dark, and there was a large crowd of mourners waiting at the gate. "Since I was not too good at walking with my cane on uneven lawns, we decided we would not go inside the cemetery to the cardinal's mausoleum that day," Paul says. "We'd visit it another time while at the family grave site." They went home, glad to have been just a small part of that memorable day.

Since the mausoleum was closed to the public during the winter, the Barkleys' next opportunity to visit came one day in April of 1997. The building sits atop the highest hill at Mount Carmel and is an attractive classic structure with stained-glass windows and a domed roof with a statue of the archangel Gabriel at the top, holding his trumpet. All of Chicago's cardinals and bishops, going back to the early days of the archdiocese, are buried there. The only entrance is a long series of stone steps leading up to the front door. "We never gave much thought to getting up there," Paul says. "Mona was there to help me, and we got to the top without a problem." There were several visitors milling around inside. Gradually, the activity died down, and when the Barkleys found themselves alone, with the sun almost setting, they decided it was time to go. They went out the door—and faced that long stone stairway.

It seemed to be steeper now, Paul thought. And there was no handrail for him to hold, to steady himself. Why hadn't he noticed before? Even with Mona's assistance, he knew he couldn't possibly get down safely. He said a quick prayer, asking for help. But a handrail did not miraculously appear.

The two looked at each other. "Maybe if I sit, and inch down one step at a time," he suggested to Mona. She was doubtful. It would be hard on Paul's back and bottom. What if he tumbled forward? But what else could they do?

Suddenly, unbelievably, a young man stood at Paul's right side. "Here," he reached for Paul. "You look like you could use some help."

Paul and Mona stared, astonished. Where had he come from? No one had been coming up the stairs, nor had anyone else been in the mausoleum. But here, as out of thin air, was this genial young man, putting his arm around Paul to steady him. Paul felt the strength of his arm. "You must be a guardian angel," he said, only half in jest. The young man smiled and gently guided Paul's first step. Mona followed, perplexed. This helper was well dressed, obviously not a workman or groundskeeper. But how had he known they needed help?

"I don't remember the details," Paul says. "I felt completely confident, as if I was in good hands. And it seems as if we got down those stairs in record time, almost gliding." They had parked in the circular driveway at the bottom of the stairs, and theirs was the only car. The young man led Paul to the car and let go of him. Paul looked up to express his gratitude, but their gracious assistant was gone. He had disappeared as silently as he had come. Mona and Paul stood stunned. Had this been a dream? Paul was safely at his car, and there was no explanation either could give. "If Mona had not witnessed this, I would have thought it was my imagination," Paul says.

But hadn't he asked God for help, there on the stairs? And wouldn't the same God who had cared for Paul all his life be listening now?

Franni Camden had worked as a grocery checkout person in Odessa, Texas, for more than sixteen years while raising three sons and becoming a grandmother. Then, in 1995, her store closed. "The manager of another store in Odessa asked some of us to come there, and we did, but the working conditions were terrible, so my son talked me into moving to Nashville, Tennessee, to start over again." It was a bittersweet request, since her son was having some marital problems and had no family anywhere in Tennessee.

Franni thought the idea had possibilities. "I don't think there's a mother alive who wouldn't want to be with her child when he's hurting." But there was a lot going on in her life. A sister was ill and might need her. Being unemployed had created financial difficulties, and it was the middle of winter—not a good time to move any-where. To make matters worse, her car was old, with a nonfunc-tioning defroster, and she doubted it would make the trip. But Franni has always been close to the Lord, and she knows he will take care of her in even her smallest need. "I love to testify of God's miracles, his mercy and grace, and his angels too!" She asked her Bible study group at Temple Baptist Church to pray about it with her, and the group discerned that she should go to Nashville, at least for a while. "Well, we have to obey the Lord," Franni says. She found a place to live in Nashville, and her son came and towed her old car there. He was extremely grateful to have his mom nearby.

Franni had been in Nashville about a week when there was an ice storm in the area. Around dinnertime, Franni's daughter-in-law, Pam, phoned to ask if Franni could pick her up from work. "I don't know the area very well," Franni protested, looking out the window at the cars sliding along. "How would I find you?"

"Well, you have to watch carefully for a little sign that says 'Training Center,'" Pam told her. "It's not a very big marker, and it's the only one. When you see it, turn into that driveway, and I'll be out in front of the building."

Franni was doubtful as she grabbed her coat and hurried to her car. It was getting dark, and the icy rain was starting to freeze. How could she drive in this weather with no defroster? And the rush-hour traffic was terrible. Franni gripped the steering wheel and tried to stay out of everyone's way. The drive seemed endless, and it took a little while before she realized that she was farther along than she should be. She had missed the sign.

Dismayed, Franni turned around, drove back a few miles, then took the same route once more. "I could hardly see out the window. Cars were skidding and honking, and I was so scared." Nor could she find any sign. Again, she realized that she had probably driven right past it. What was she going to do? How could she find this tiny marker in the midst of rain and traffic?

"I hunted for that sign, but it was nowhere. I kept praying and crying out to the Lord to help me. And about the fourth or fifth time I passed the same intersection, I saw something ahead that was . . . different."

As she approached, she realized that it was a sign. An enormous metal sign, at least five feet by five feet, painted a vivid green as all the major highway signs are. But this sign did not give route or highway directions. Instead, huge letters spelled the words *training center,* and a giant arrow pointed to the now obvious driveway. It was her sign, the one she had been looking for—no one could have missed it. But this sign was not tiny, as Pam had described it. And Franni had driven this stretch of road several times that night; she had gone right past this driveway. There had been no sign there before.

Franni brought her daughter-in-law safely home that night. She eventually settled into Nashville and supported her son through a difficult two years. Eventually, the young couple did break up, and the time seemed right for her to return to Odessa, where she now is a grocery clerk again. Life is usually good, but when it isn't, Franni can think back to that very special night in the rain, when she saw the huge green sign as a guidepost from the angels?

How does Franni know it came from heaven? Because her job in Nashville took her past that driveway every day thereafter, and the only sign she ever saw there was the small one Pam had described. "God made a big old sign just for me, just for that night," Franni says. "And he sent the angels to put it up."

When Anthony Thomas Guarino was born, no one was happier than his grandpa, Tom Vallombroso. In Italy, where Tom was born, custom dictates that the first grandson is special and carries part of his grandfather's name. The Guarino and Vallombroso families lived in Astonia, Connecticut, but tradition ran deep. Sadly, Tom could only imagine what this little package of joy looked like. He had lost his sight at age fifty-six to retinitis pigmentosa and cataracts. But he needn't have worried; the bond between the two was instant.

Baby Tony had several health problems and was in and out of hospitals during those first few years. "My dad was the only one I could talk to about the medical issues," says Judy Guarino, Tony's mom. "The rest of the family was too scared to listen, but Dad always did, asking very good questions, even suggesting some to ask the doctors." Perhaps because of his own difficulties, Tom was extrasensitive to Tony's.

By the time Tony was three, he and Grandpa regularly watched together *Wheel of Fortune, Jeopardy,* and the news. "Tony loved to snuggle with Dad in their favorite chair during these shows," says Judy. "Tony would describe what he was seeing so that Dad could feel like he was seeing it too. After school, the bus would drop Tony off at Grandpa's house while they waited for me to come home from work. This went on for years."

As Tony's ninth birthday approached, Tom began to ask a special favor from God. He said nothing to anyone about it, but with the help of some family members he purchased a special toy for his grandson, a big noisy police car that Tony had been wanting. During that time Tom's wife also took him to his ophthalmologist for a routine checkup. The doctor dilated Tom's eyes as always to check how his disease was progressing, then left Tom and his wife, Norma, alone as the drops took effect.

Norma was reading a magazine when Tom asked, "Norma, does the clock on the wall say 3:00 P.M.?"

Norma looked up. "Yes, but how do you know that?"

"I don't know how to explain it," Tom told her. "But I can see!"

Norma shouted for the doctor, who had no explanation. Perhaps it was the drops? He decided to keep Tom on them for a while and see what happened.

When Tom and Norma returned home, still in a state of shock, the first person to greet them was Tony. "Nice shirt, Tony," Grandpa said. "But how come you have that long tail of hair in the back?"

"It's just a fad, Grandpa," Tony told him. "But who told you about it?"

Grandpa turned to Judy. "Now *you* need a touch-up!" he said, laughing. Judy's skin started to tingle. It was true—her roots were showing.

Tony looked at Tom's big grin. "Grandpa!" he shouted. "You can see!"

It was mid-October, and Tom became reacquainted with the world during the weeks leading up to Tony's ninth birthday. Everything seemed new again, each day a gift. On that special afternoon, Tom watched with glee as Tony blew out his birthday candles and opened his very special gift, the police car from Grandpa. It was the best day either of them had ever had.

The next day, however, brought consternation with it. Once again, Tom's sight was gone, and once again no one knew why. Tony was very upset. He had brought Tom a picture he had taken, and Tom had to admit he couldn't see it. Why had this happened to the man he loved so much?

But Tom, as always, had the explanation. "Several months ago, I asked God for something special," he told his grandson as they cuddled together in their favorite chair. "I asked him if he would let me see you just once in my life, maybe on the day when you turned nine years old."

"You did?" Tony asked, wiping away tears.

"Yes." Tom nodded. "I wanted to see you open that special gift. And God didn't just give me one day. He sent angels to lend me their eyes, so I could see you all month. Instead of being sad about that, Tony, we should be happy!"

Tony understood. "Every day he thanked Dad's angels for their gift," Judy says. "He continued to share his life with Dad and snuggled even closer while they watched TV together."

Tom would never attend another party for Tony. He died five months later. But his family knows he is watching over them now with the eyes only heaven can provide.

⁂

Gloria Manning grew up in the Pocono Mountains in Pennsylvania and was an "outdoor girl" from the moment she learned to walk. Even after she raised a family, became a widow, and finally became a senior citizen, she still walked. This was fortunate, because she now lived in an apartment complex in Willow Grove, Pennsylvania, mainly rented by younger people who were gone all day; there was no one there to give her a ride. Until her retirement at age seventy-four, Gloria walked to and from work, a distance of about three-quarters of a mile each way. It was just part of her routine.

After work on a beautiful fall day, Gloria gathered her purse and belongings, waved good-bye to her coworkers, and started the trek home. "The road has no sidewalks," she says, "and as I passed a corner, a car came around it very fast." Trying to get out of the way, Gloria hopped on the grass and dislodged a stone. Tripping over it, she lost her balance and fell, facedown, onto the concrete street. Pain invaded her face, her glasses fell off, and her dentures broke. Part of them jammed into the roof of her mouth. The car zoomed by.

Gloria lay on the street, bruised, bleeding, and dazed; her slacks were torn at the knees. Blood from her mouth dripped onto the cement. What was she going to do? She had a distance yet to go—could she make it in this condition? Shakily, she attempted to get to a kneeling position. Just then she heard another vehicle approach.

Not again! The driver wouldn't see her there and would run over her! Gloria was about to scream when the vehicle pulled alongside her and stopped. It was a rickety truck, and a man was getting out of it, carrying a roll of paper towels. How unusual. Gloria looked up at him, and caught her breath. "To me, he looked just like Jesus, with long hair and a quiet calmness about him." In a moment he was at her side, handing her some towels for her bleeding mouth and nose. "Without saying a word, he picked up my glasses and purse, and helped me into his truck."

With a lurch, the wobbly vehicle started up. Gloria closed her eyes for a moment. Was she safe here? She thought of the man's beautiful face and somehow knew she had nothing to fear. How had he seen her, lying there on the side of the road? It was a miracle that he hadn't driven over her.

Gloria's apartment complex was ahead just a few blocks, but before she had time to direct him, the man turned in at the gate. As if he had driven the route a thousand times, he went up one street, turned at another, and finally stopped in front of Gloria's building. With the engine still running, the man came over to Gloria's side, opened the door, lifted her down, carried her to her front hall, and handed her purse to her. "Can you get up your steps OK?" he asked. It was the first time he had spoken.

Gloria's mouth was still bleeding, so all she could do was nod. Turning away, she painfully climbed her stairs, listening for the sound of the truck rattling away. The sound never came. By the time Gloria had reached the welcome safety of her apartment and her front window, the truck had disappeared.

Gloria went straight to the kitchen sink. "I don't know how I did it—because I have a condition that makes me faint at the sight of blood—but I pulled the broken dentures from the roof of my mouth. Then I put ice cubes in my mouth and phoned my daughter."

Luckily, two weeks before, Gloria had been fitted for new dentures. They were ready the very next day, and although Gloria needed to heal before wearing them, she was able to go back to work when the time came. But first, as she quieted from the shock, she thought about her experience. And the more she thought about it, the stranger it seemed.

For one thing, the man had never asked Gloria where she lived, and her apartment was not the easiest place to find. For another, although the truck was quite loud, she never heard it leave. "The fact that he looked like depictions of Jesus I've seen, and he came immediately, and he had paper towels in his truck—I am convinced he was an angel sent to me by God. I was so sorry there was no way to thank him."

But she thinks he knows.

THE DAY THE ANGELS DROVE

I just prayed for their guardian angels to pull them through.
I knew they'd fight, fight to the bitter end.

—A FORMER COAL MINER, AFTER NINE COMRADES WERE RESCUED FROM A
MINE CAVE-IN IN SOMERSET COUNTY, PENNSYLVANIA

As we've seen, many people work in jobs where angelic protection seems necessary. Cross-country truck drivers probably fall into this category, and Gail Backlund would agree.

On a gorgeous spring day, Gail could feel the sun on her left arm as she pulled out of the truck yard in Tulsa, Oklahoma. Her assignment was a fairly routine day-and-a-half trip to Springfield, Illinois, hauling a load of corrosives in her fifty-foot trailer. It was dangerous cargo, but Gail was a professional who had logged many miles, and she was well qualified for the job. There was an extra bonus today: another driver, Tommy, was going to Springfield too, carrying the same cargo.

"It's always nice to have a buddy along on these jobs," Gail says. "The time goes by much faster, and that person is always available should anything go wrong."

Tommy was first out of the gate, and Gail was about five miles behind him on the road. Soon, the two were talking on their CB radios and enjoying the day.

As the big rigs turned onto a two-lane highway, they began to build up speed. Eventually both were traveling at more than ninety miles per hour. "That speed was not unusual," Gail admits, "because as a professional tractor-trailer driver, I normally drove at least twenty miles over the speed limit. Even though it was a dangerous speed, I felt that I could handle any situation that might occur."

The first two hours on the road passed without incident. Gail appreciated the weather. In earlier days, she might have said a small prayer of thanks to God for loving her and keeping her safe. But life had handed Gail some blows, and although she had been raised a Christian, those days were over. "I believed that God existed, but that he didn't care about me. I had given up the church and put God behind me." Instead, she chatted with Tommy, who stayed about five miles ahead.

Another hour went by. Suddenly, without warning, Tommy began yelling over the CB radio. "Oh my God!" he shouted. "I can't stop!"

"Tommy!" Gail grabbed her radio. "What's happening?"

"My God!" he shouted again. "I'm going to hit them!"

"Tommy, Tommy . . ." Gail couldn't see him, she could only hear his terrified voice. She shouted again, but there was no response.

Just then, Gail reached the top of a steep grade, a vantage point from which she could see the long, thin ribbon of highway unfolding in front of her. Yes, there was Tommy way ahead of her—or at least the back of his trailer. What was wrong? "Tommy!" she shouted again, but heard nothing.

Alarmed, Gail started the long descent, her speed building. "About halfway down, I got a better look and could see that Tommy's brakes were smoking, and he was driving all over the road." His brakes must be out! Now Gail could see that there was at least one gas station ahead of Tommy. If he hit those gasoline pumps . . . Immediately Gail reached for her Jake Brake switch.

"A Jake Brake slows a diesel engine down faster than air brakes can, letting a truck stop sooner and safer," Gail explains. "But nothing happened! I turned the switch off, then on again. Still nothing. My Jake Brake wasn't working!" Gail glanced at the speed gauge. She was traveling about 110 miles per hour. As she looked ahead, she realized there was not one but two gas stations, one on either side of the road.

Gail's load was combustible. There was going to be a terrible wreck ahead—Tommy, the gas-station fuel, customers, other drivers—unless she could do something to stop it. Desperate, she stood on the tractor's brake pedal and pulled the separate handle to ignite the truck brakes, but the truck would not slow down. It had been years since Gail prayed. But now she heard herself screaming. "Lord, help me! I can't stop!"

Now at closer range, she could see that Tommy had managed to stop his truck about one hundred yards past the gas stations, but he was stuck in the middle of the road. Gail was still traveling around ninety miles an hour and wouldn't have room to go around him. If she crashed into him, if their combustible loads met, she didn't want to think about the inferno that would result. *Should I aim for one of the gas stations?* she wondered, panic now taking hold.

"Lord, help me! Send your angels!" Gail prayed again, as she stood on her brake pedal with both feet. She was less than half a mile now from the gas stations and still going eighty miles per hour. Should she swerve to the left and try to turn her rig around so she would be facing uphill? The trailer might tip, but at least she would save some lives. Did she have time and room to turn? Gail took another look at the gas station. What was that vehicle parked by a pump? Her heart seemed to stop. It was a yellow school bus, filled with children.

Oh, God, no. If she couldn't make the turn, if she lost control, her rig would end up there. The children were right in her path. She imagined the explosions, the carnage and death. "Oh, angels, *please!*" she cried and, still standing on the brake pedal, tried to turn the steering wheel.

"At that exact moment, the wheel jerked out of my hands!" Gail says. "I tried to grab it again, but I couldn't. I was now so close to the gas pump and the bus that I could clearly see a little girl sitting in the backseat pointing at me." The truck turned back to the left, missing the pumps and the school bus by inches. But Gail's hands were not on the steering wheel. How had the truck turned by itself?

Now she was bouncing straight across the road, toward the other gas station. Again, Gail tried to grab the wheel. The truck was slowing slightly, and maybe she could turn it around. But again, the wheel was jerked out of her hands. *God, God.* There were at least seven cars parked at or near the gas pumps there. "Get out of the way!" Gail screamed at the people. "You're going to get blown up!"

As she got closer, she realized that no one was moving. They were all standing in place, a few even holding gas hoses. "Some had their heads bowed, as if they were praying. Others were just looking at me, their faces stunned." It made no sense, but again Gail seemed unable to take the wheel.

Watching helplessly, Gail saw her truck begin to turn by itself. "It was as if someone else was driving. I looked out the front windshield but I couldn't see anything. Something seemed to be blocking my view." She felt the presence of unseen hands holding the steering wheel, maneuvering it away from danger. Then Gail could see again. Somehow, her rig had passed the second station without mishap! But she was not safe yet. Looming ahead of her was the ditch, running along the side of the road. If the truck lurched into the ditch, it would probably turn over and spill its contents.

Yet, unbelievably, the truck turned again, away from the road's edge. "It was then that I realized what was happening," Gail says. "Angels were driving my truck! I had nothing to fear, because I was in the hands of the messengers from God." Tommy's rig loomed in front of her now, the final obstacle on what was becoming a miracle journey. "Lord," Gail prayed, "stop me—now!"

The truck came to a complete stop, just two feet from Tommy's bumper. In shock, Gail climbed out of her cab and knelt on the ground in thanks. Then, as she looked up, she gasped. Angels, angels all around her. "They emerged from my truck and came closer to where I was kneeling. I could only see their shadows, but they were the most beautiful beings." She felt as if the whole of heaven was there, surrounding everyone for miles around. Bits of Psalm 23 came to her mind from an earlier time: *Yea, though I walk through the valley of the shadow of death, I will fear no evil.* For the first time in years, she praised the Lord.

Gradually, she realized that she was not the only one kneeling on the side of the two-lane highway. "At least fifty people had assembled there, gas-station customers and the children from the school bus, all kneeling and praying, and Tommy was right beside me, praying louder than anyone. Tommy had never believed in God—not until that day." The entire group, strangers to one another, sang in thanksgiving. It was an amazing moment, one that would be difficult to explain later to those who hadn't been there to witness it.

Gradually and quietly, people got up, drifted to their cars and drove off, some still dazed. Gail, Tommy, and the little girl from the school bus were the last at the scene. "I noticed that the girl was staring at my truck cab and waving," Gail says. "I guessed that she was still seeing the angels." Gail put her arm around the child and walked with her back to the bus. The driver had come out to look for her.

"That was the finest piece of driving I ever saw!" he said to Gail.

The child knew better. "It was the angels! Everyone knows they're the best drivers in the whole world!"

Angelic appearances are not usually charted on a truck driver's log when a run has ended. But this event is written in Gail's heart, where she can remember it at will. She knows now that although we forget about God, he will never forget about us. She praises him daily, and gives thanks.

Voice in the Fire

Angels are speaking to all of us . . . some of us are only listening better.
—Anonymous

᭗᭜᭗

Mark is a volunteer firefighter in west-central Ohio. "The responsibilities of a volunteer firefighter are mostly the same as a career firefighter," Mark says, "except we are not on duty." The volunteers meet once a month for training and a general business meeting. If a fire breaks out, anyone who's in town goes to the station to get the truck, and the others proceed directly to the scene. Everyone is trained to enter, search and rescue, ventilate the roof, and operate the pump, among other tasks. In addition, Mark is a paramedic, the only one in his district. He can use a defibrillator, give drugs, place a breathing tube, and administer an IV.

Recently, the fire alarm sounded regarding an unoccupied mobile home. When Mark got to the scene, few firefighters had arrived, and the structure was blazing. He decided to go in.

"My partner and I entered through the back door of the trailer," Mark says (firefighters always travel in pairs). "We kept low to the floor to avoid any superheated gasses that might be higher up." Mark had control of the hose nozzle, and his partner was helping drag the hose. Mark saw an orange glow, directed the nozzle toward it, and put out that part of the fire easily. The men crawled through a doorway into a second room filled with furniture and items lying all around.

"Being in a fire is nothing like what they show on TV," Mark says. "If you are lucky, you might be able to see the hose you are carrying. But the smoke is so thick that everything else is done by touch, and of course you are wearing heavy leather gloves." It was extremely difficult to see, but eventually Mark located the source of the flames and directed water at it. But the flames kept coming back. "This told us that the fire was being fueled by something other than solid material—like propane or heating oil."

It is still possible, Mark says, to contain the spread of such a fire by shutting off the fuel supply or wetting down the materials around the fire. Mark assumed that the men now gathering outside the trailer had already turned off the fuel supply, so he and his partner opted to stay inside and keep watering the flames. "It was about this time that I began to feel uneasy."

At first it was just a sense that something wasn't right. Mark thought it was his imagination, but the feeling persisted. Then he heard a clear voice: "Mark," it said, "You need to go." Mark was astonished. The voice was audible, definitely male, with no accent. It couldn't be his partner. He was too far away to be heard. Nor were there any openings in the trailer where someone outside could yell through. And an air pack distorts a voice—"it's kind of a Darth Vader effect"—not like the voice he was hearing now, which was so definite and intimate that it was almost at his ear. On an instinctive level, Mark recognized that it was "one I could trust and obey." But who was it, and where was it coming from?

Mark kept working. A few moments later, he heard the message again. "OK," Mark said (in his mind) to the voice. "I'll go pretty soon. Let me hit this a little more and see if I can get somewhere."

The voice was not convinced. "Mark!" it answered, in a no-nonsense tone. "You need to go *now!*" The voice did not sound angry that he had been ignoring it. "It sounded as if it was just giving me an urgent warning, like a father would speak to his child." Mark could disregard the command no longer. He turned, motioned to his partner, and the two crouched down to make their way back to the first room. It was hard going because of all the debris strewn around.

As they reached the first room, Mark saw flames and realized that a flashover was coming—something that all firefighters dread. It can happen when the contents of a room are so hot that they explode, engulfing a room in seconds. "Gear might keep you alive for a minute if you are caught in a flashover," Mark says, "but you will still be seriously burned." (In fact, the survival rate for firefighters caught in a flashover is only about 4 percent.)

"Get down! Get down!" Mark yelled as his partner hit the floor. Mark aimed water at the flash flame and drove it back just enough for the two to scramble out the door. Had they still been in the second room—or in the first room for just a few more seconds—they probably would have been badly injured, or worse.

Outside now, as the fire waned, Mark thought more seriously about the voice. Oddly, it seemed as if he had heard it before. Yes—now he remembered. He had been seventeen when he lost control of a van as he braked to avoid hitting a deer. The vehicle had rolled over a fence and landed on its top. Mark had assumed he would die within a few minutes, but he had heard a voice reassuring him: "Wait and see how this plays out." Mark had pushed away his panic and sustained only a few cuts as he crawled to safety.

But who was the voice? After the trailer fire, Mark thought about it. Finally he told a friend—another firefighter—about his experience. This man had served more than two tours of duty in Vietnam as a ranger extensively involved in combat, and he had served a stint in Desert Storm. He immediately knew what Mark was describing. "I heard that voice on a number of occasions, in fires and in combat," the veteran told Mark, "and I learned to listen to it. The times I got hurt were when I didn't."

Mark doesn't think he will ever forget this experience. Every now and then, when he sees a sunset or steps outside on a crisp winter morning, he says, "I thank God that I am still around to experience these things. I personally believe that I owe my life to whoever's voice that was, maybe God, maybe an angel, I don't know. But I'm sure glad he was on my entry team."

LOVE FOR ALWAYS

The Lord is close to the brokenhearted,
and those who are crushed in spirit, he saves.

—PSALM 34:19 NAB

I t had seemed like a sensible idea at the time: a trip to London to soothe her sorrow. Margo Fallis was a wife and mother of five, living in Salt Lake City. But she had been born in Edinburgh, Scotland, and had countless relatives scattered throughout the British Isles. This extended family knew that Margo and her husband had recently adopted a baby girl named Brooke, their sixth child, and that unexpectedly the birth mother had changed her mind and taken the baby back. They understood that although Christmas was approaching and Margo had much to do, she needed to mourn. They had welcomed her, wrapped her in wordless sympathy, given her comfort and space, and eventually put her on the plane home.

As eagerly as she had gone, Margo was now counting the hours until she arrived in Salt Lake City. She had been through several time zones since leaving Gatwick Airport seven hours ago, and she was tired and cranky—and ravenous. There was nothing hearty to eat during the airplane ride, so she had nibbled on a salad. She felt shaky, as if she could cry at any moment, and she missed her family. Worse, instead of continuing its straight and reassuring journey across the Midwestern plains, the huge jet had run into bad weather and had circled above Atlanta for almost an hour. Ultimately, the pilot explained that all flights were being canceled. They would land in Atlanta and resume their flight when the fog cleared.

It was the worst possible scenario. Margo had spent every cent of English money she still had during her last day in London, never thinking she would need any cash. And she didn't own a credit card—at that time, she just didn't believe in them. "Now here I was in Atlanta, with thousands of other stranded people, and I didn't have a cent." Nor did the airlines offer any assistance. Her hunger pangs mixed with tension and worry as she and the other passengers dragged their luggage down the tarmac to the airline waiting-room area. What was she going to do?

Margo called her family collect and explained the situation. Afterward, she found a seat at an unused gate. But as time passed and her hunger increased, she grew restless. "Out of frustration, I began to walk around," she recalls. At one point, dragging her luggage along, she went into a restroom and said a desperate prayer. "I prayed that the fog would lift, that I wouldn't be scared, and that they would hurry up and let me go home." Tears of frustration spilled down her checks, and she let them come. Then, after wiping her face with a paper towel, she walked back to her gate. No miracle had happened. The fog was still a thick gray blanket covering every window. Passengers were curled up on the uncomfortable chairs, some trying to sleep, others reading, a few eating. Margo's stomach rumbled, and she felt close to tears again. Instead she sat down and tried to think of something pleasant.

Only a few moments had passed when a middle-aged man sat down in the seat next to Margo. "He smiled at me," she says. "He had beautiful blue eyes that sparkled, and neatly combed light brown hair. I made an effort to smile back, but it was obvious how miserable I was."

"Where are you headed?" the stranger asked.

"Salt Lake City," Margo murmured.

"Really? I'm going there too." Had he noticed her weary sadness? His gaze seemed to hold both concern and compassion, and he was obviously trying to cheer her up.

"We started a nice easy conversation. He told me his name was Andrew. He never asked my name, but when he suggested we go for a walk, I didn't feel hesitant. For some reason I felt I could trust him." The pair strolled around the airport, Andrew carrying one of her suitcases, and enjoyed the Christmas decorations and the carols playing through the loudspeakers.

Andrew's presence was immensely reassuring. "He promised he'd stay with me the whole time and make sure I got on the plane safely," Margo says. She felt strangely calmed by his kind reassurance. "He even seemed somewhat familiar to me, but when I asked him, he assured me we'd never met." Margo's hard knot of anxiety and grief began to soften.

The hours passed pleasantly. At one point Andrew wandered off and soon returned with food for both of them. Margo had never tasted anything more delicious than this stale ham sandwich and bottle of water! "We talked about everything," she says, "but mostly about me and what was going on in my life. I found myself telling him all about Brooke and then my other children. He asked about my parents and my adventurous life, living in so many different places." Andrew's reaction to the lost baby was reassuring. "He told me I should love the children I had at home and that things like losing Brooke happen for a reason—that one day I might understand it better." Oddly, she thought she might. Her broken spirit, which had caused her such pain for so long, seemed oddly soothed.

Finally, six hours later, the fog lifted and it was time to reboard the airplane. Margo could hardly believe that so much time had passed. She felt by now as if Andrew were a lifelong friend, and she could hardly wait to introduce him to the family members who would be waiting for her in Salt Lake City. Andrew took her up to the ticket attendant and watched as she started down the ramp.

"I'll be right behind you," he called. "Good-bye, Margo."

"Good-bye," she called back. Odd—she didn't recall telling him her first name. But she was too tired for thought now, and she collapsed into her seat and fell asleep. She was perfectly safe. Andrew was on the plane.

When the plane touched down in Salt Lake City, Margo was almost the first one off. Her family was waiting there, and her children hugged her in welcome. "Wait until you meet the wonderful guardian angel who helped me in Atlanta. He was so nice, and he'll be coming out soon." Margo waited as everyone deplaned, waited until the last passenger had exited. But Andrew never appeared.

Puzzled, she led the family to the luggage-pickup area, but there was no sign of him there either. Had he changed his travel plans at the very last minute? But no, he had promised he would take care of her. Margo was confused and disappointed; she would not be able to introduce this dear man to her children.

The days passed quickly. One morning, Margo's mother phoned. "I've just received a package of old photographs from our relatives in Scotland. Come and see!" Margo excitedly rushed over.

The women sat and looked through the photos. Margo's mother pointed out Margo's great uncle Jimmy, her grandpa Crawford, her great-grandma Geddes, and many more. Then Margo reached into the pile, pulled out a photograph at random, and gasped. Chills ran up her spine.

Margo's mother took the photo and looked on the back of it, where the identity of the man was written: "Andrew Donaldson, Shetland Islands, 1897." "This was your great-grandfather," her mother said.

"Yes," Margo nodded, tears spilling down her face. She knew this man, even though he had died long before she was born. He was Andrew, the man at the airport who seemed so familiar to her, who had shown her such kindness, compassion, and comfort. Not a guardian angel after all, but a saint doing an angel's work. She would not be alone, he had told her, and now she understood. Where there is love, even across the centuries, there is healing.

Margo kissed the photograph. "Thank you, Grandpa Andrew," she whispered. "I love you too."

A MIRACLE FOR RITA

The very presence of an angel is a communication.
Even when an angel crosses our path in silence, God has said to us,
"I am here. I am present in your life."

—TOBIAS PALMER

Sister Mary Raphael lay back in bed, trying to absorb what the doctor had just told her: multiple sclerosis! She had a serious disease, one that might take her life.

Nuns, of course, were supposed to be peacefully prepared for death at all times. They were so saintly and close to heaven—at least that's what outsiders thought. But Sister Mary Raphael hadn't considered the possibility that she might die at this age. She was twenty-three and had only begun to live.

Raised in a large Catholic family in Iowa, Rita McLaughlin was gifted and rambunctious. She loved God deeply and wanted to be a nun. In 1955, at age fifteen—overruling the judgment of her parents and some of the sisters—she joined the Servite novitiate, moved to the convent, and finished high school through a home-schooling program. The order demanded strict discipline and sacrifice, but Rita thrived on it, and her prayer life deepened. What joy to be so close to God, to spend every waking moment serving him! At age seventeen, she received the full habit and was given the name Sister Mary Raphael in honor of the archangel Raphael, which would prove a significant choice.

Sister Mary Raphael had just celebrated her twentieth birthday and was happily teaching school when she began noticing odd physical symptoms. "I started dropping things and tripping, and twice I completely lost my vision." Her physician found nothing wrong.

"Just get a lot of rest," he told her, "and work on ruling your symptoms instead of letting them rule you."

Sister Mary Raphael obeyed and had almost forgotten the episodes when, after a bout with flu in 1963, her right knee began to give way at unexpected times. "I compensated by always walking near a wall so I could grab something when it happened." There were strange bouts of numbness and waves of fatigue. She coped quietly, but one morning as she walked across the playground, her entire right side collapsed and she fell. She could ignore her symptoms no longer.

A surgeon operated on Sister Mary Raphael's unsteady right knee, inserted pins to hold her kneecap in place, and compressed her knee into a cast. He ordered therapy for the left knee too, since it was beginning to atrophy. Then he sat down with her to explain this difficult diagnosis.

Although there is no definitive test to diagnose multiple sclerosis, doctors know that it is a disease of the central nervous system in which the sheathing that covers nerves develops lesions. Eventually scar tissue begins to block the nerve passages, distorting messages the brain sends to the body or preventing signals from completing their circuits. A small percentage of those afflicted experience permanent remission. For the majority, the journey is slow and painful as the disease gets progressively worse.

Now, as the doctor left, Sister Mary Raphael fought fear and bewilderment. Why would God allow this to happen to her? Hadn't she given her life to him?

Yes, she thought. *And my life is his to do with whatever he decides.* The reassuring habit of prayer, which had stood her in such good stead during other times, helped her rise to this challenge too. There was nothing to worry about. God would take care of her.

Time passed, and Sister Mary Raphael's condition worsened. Both her physician and a priest spiritual adviser suggested that she leave the convent and return to life in the world. They pointed out that her work schedule was physically demanding and created stress that she couldn't handle. Ultimately, she would need more medical care than a convent setting could provide. Spiritually, she had most likely taken her vows at too young an age (today it would not be permitted) and did not have the wisdom then to understand the commitment she was making.

Initially, Sister Mary Raphael refused to listen to either her doctor or her spiritual adviser. She told them adamantly that she had freely chosen this life. Besides, no one could say *for sure* that she even had multiple sclerosis. But as she prayed for guidance, she underwent a change of heart. "My prayer became 'Make your will known to me, and make it so clear that I will never doubt it for the rest of my life.'"

Ultimately, Sister Mary Raphael recognized God's direction. The signs were obvious, and in the summer of 1968 she officially resumed life as Rita McLaughlin, teaching special-education children in a school near Pittsburgh. Her multiple sclerosis also went into remission. For the first time in years, Rita felt healthy and strong. She missed convent life but was ready to see what else God had planned for her.

Three years later, Rita changed her name again, when she married Ronald Klaus. Although she had not been consciously seeking a mate, God had apparently found one for her—even though he was Lutheran!—and she had no doubt that this was the proper next step. There was just one problem: her new husband knew, of course, that she had been a nun for many years. But Rita didn't tell him about her medical situation. "I convinced myself there was no reason to do so," she admits. "Why should I burden Ron with worries over things that might never happen?" During the next several years, Rita's good health continued. She gave birth to three daughters without experiencing any problems during her pregnancies or afterward. Obviously she was one of the lucky ones, in permanent remission. She thanked God every night.

Then, in 1978, Rita's nightmare began again, at first with constant fatigue, which she attributed to the demands of three preschoolers. Then she began to stumble. One day she almost dropped her infant and then had an episode of complete paralysis. Stunned, Ron brought her to the doctor. "What could be happening?" he asked.

Rita was afraid to answer, for, of course, she knew. That night, Rita told her husband what she should have told him long before they married. When she was finished, Ron looked at her. "Is that *all* of it?" he asked. Rita nodded.

"I want a divorce," Ron said. He slammed out of the house and drove away.

Sitting there in the darkness, Rita faced the enormity of what she had done. "So completely had I rejected the fact that I might have multiple sclerosis, it never occurred to me that my dishonesty might one day cost me my marriage." Now she faced the prospect of being left alone as her health deteriorated. Worse was the injustice she had done to Ron. They had agreed from the start that divorce would never be an option, but now she couldn't blame him for his decision.

When Ron did return, however, he had calmed down. "It hurts that you didn't think you could trust me," he told her quietly. "But now we've got to figure out the best way to help you."

They didn't have much time, because things went downhill quickly during the next months. Rita began to experience excruciating pain, particularly in her right leg, where deteriorating muscles were causing bones to press on the sciatic nerve. When the pain finally became unbearable, her surgeon severed all the muscles and tendons behind her knee, sliding the kneecap around to the side and permanently disfiguring her leg. From now on she could walk only with calipers and leg braces. Her life had changed forever, not only physically but also spiritually.

Rita was furious with God. It had started slowly, just skipping prayer time when she felt anxious or upset. Then her estrangement grew. *Why have you done this to me?* she stormed, over and over. *Why did you have me leave the convent, give me a husband and three children, then make it impossible for me to be a wife and mother?* No answer came, and eventually Rita stopped asking. There was nothing more to say. God had abandoned her. She hated him with all her heart.

"My hostility and bitterness worsened, until it spilled out on everyone," Rita recalls. "Brick by brick, I built a wall between Ron and me, part of it based on the guilt I felt for deceiving him, part on anger because I was now totally dependent on him." Her daughters pulled away as well, preferring to spend time with anyone but their mom. Since therapy and whirlpool sessions and electroshock to stimulate remaining muscles were not covered by insurance, the family's debts mounted. The girls received subsidized lunches at school. Never in her life had Rita felt so humiliated or alone.

One evening a friend phoned. "Rita, there's a healing service tonight at St. Ferdinand's. Would you like to go?"

Rita was incredulous. "*Healing,* in this modern age? Like those charlatans on television? I don't believe in that."

"Well, that was the way I felt too, but—"

"No, I do *not* want to go." Rita looked up. Ron was standing there.

"I want you to go, Rita," he said.

"No!" She didn't want to be a spectacle in front of others. Besides, she hated God, and she wasn't going to ask him for anything, ever again.

Her husband was almost pleading. "We've been to every doctor on earth, and none of them can heal you. What harm can this do?"

Rita was silent. She had put Ron through a lot. And if this Lutheran man wanted her to go to a Catholic healing service, it was the least she could do. But no one was going to get her up in front of a bunch of people or pray over her. Absolutely no one.

St. Ferdinand's was jammed when they arrived, and Rita's friend joined her family after settling Rita in the back. However, a young usher saw Rita and propelled her to a pew up front, despite her protests. Almost at once, the crowd—everyone but Rita—began singing "Abba, Father" ("God was not my Father anymore," she points out), and a procession of priests came down the center aisle. All passed but one, who suddenly stopped behind Rita. "Wait!" she heard him say to the others, and then from behind her, she felt him putting his arms around her in a "backward bear hug."

No! She didn't want any attention! And why was he doing this now, instead of at the end of the ceremony, which was the customary time for healing prayer? There was no place to hide, and Rita turned crimson as the other priests, people in the pew, everyone in church, it seemed, elevated their hands and rained prayer over her.

"And then, all of a sudden, an explosion of peace filled me, inside and out," Rita says. "I had never felt so loved in all my life, and I heard myself praying for the first time in years." Throughout the service her heart grew lighter and warmer. When the evening ended, the serenity stayed. It went home with her. It filled every crack in her heart and her life. In an instant, all her anger and despair had gone. "I was still crippled on the outside, but inside I was whole."

Rita's physical condition continued to deteriorate. She now wore full-length steel braces on both legs, used her wheelchair frequently, and drove a car with hand controls. Her 1985 checkup revealed lost bowel and bladder control, partial paralysis and atrophy of all four limbs, spasticity (involuntary muscle contractions), and more. The doctor told her that there no longer was a chance that she would go into remission. At most, she would live another three to five years. Despite the grim prognosis, Rita's buoyant spirit continued, tempered only with bouts of grieving for the hurt she had caused her family. Everyone noticed the change in her. "If I had to choose between a spiritual or a physical healing," she told Ron one day, "I'd take what I have been given. There's no substitute for inner peace."

In June of 1986, Rita was taking a Scripture class. On June 18, she had a particularly bad physical day and fell into bed, exhausted. It was hot in the bedroom, and Rita couldn't sleep. She was thinking about something she had recently heard. Many people believed that Mary, the Mother of Jesus, was appearing in Medjugorje, in then Yugoslavia, to several peasant children. Healings and spiritual conversions seemed to be happening there in record numbers. How Rita longed to go! But such a trip would be impossible. And obviously, a physical healing was not in God's plan for her.

Now, as Rita lay in the darkened bedroom, she heard a gentle voice. "Why don't you *ask?*" it said. Startled, Rita looked around. The radio was off, no one had come in. Yet, the voice had been real. Could it have been her guardian angel? Or possibly Mary, the

Mother of Jesus? Actually, did it matter who was delivering this message if it was from God, her Father? Unexpected words came to her. "Mary," she whispered, "please ask your Son to heal me, in any way I need to be healed."

Immediately, electricity coursed through her, like tingling champagne bubbles, particularly strong on her right side. It was so comfortable! Amazed and blissful, Rita fell asleep.

She awakened the next morning almost an hour late, with no memory of the previous night's events. She would miss her class! Ron settled her in the car and cautioned her against speeding. Rita agreed, then shot out of the driveway.

The helper assigned to Rita had left, so she was wheeled into her class, late, by a cafeteria worker. And because she had skipped breakfast, she now had a caffeine-withdrawal headache. Since Rita couldn't hold a pen anymore, she tried to listen carefully, but the headache was a painful distraction. She could hardly wait until coffee-break time.

At ten o'clock as the others filed out, Rita suddenly felt a rush of heat roar through her, from her toes to the top of her head. What was happening? Then she began to itch everywhere, like a million pinpricks. She reached down to scratch her right leg and almost screamed. She could feel her fingers on the leg! She could feel her toes moving, the inside of her shoes, the braces! Yet Rita had felt no sensations below her knees for several years!

How could this be? Afraid to tell anyone, Rita kept silent during the rest of class, and then drove home quickly—because she had to use the bathroom! Ron would not be there at this time. Could she get out of the van alone, get into the house? She had not attempted that in months. Now, however, she ascended without even breathing hard. And when she raised her skirt to unlock her braces, she saw her right leg.

"My God, my God!" Rita screamed. She could hardly believe her eyes. The kneecap was back on top of her knee where it absolutely could not be! Her permanently deformed right leg was now perfectly normal. (Her physician would later discover that all the severed ligaments and muscles behind her knee had been reattached and restored.) Nor was any other part of her spastic or paralyzed or atrophied. Laying her crutches on the floor, Rita ran through the house, weeping and praising God. In an instant, her body—and her life—had been completely restored.

The congregation watched in hushed awe as the Klaus family walked down the church aisle that following Sunday. Was it just a coincidence that the Gospel, selected many months ago and read in all Catholic churches around the world that day, was about Jesus healing the crippled man? Rita did not think so.

But God had more in store for her. As word spread, she accepted a few invitations to speak about her healing. She felt compelled to share but uneasy about going too far away. During this time, she also attended a conference on angels. "I learned there that the archangel Raphael—who I was named after in the convent—was the patron of healings and of travel. It was a real sign for me; God had taken me through a healing and he would guard me on the road as well. I had always been under his—and Raphael's—protection, even when I didn't know or believe it."

Rita realized that God's love for her had never changed. His plan, which at times had seemed so wrong, had been right after all. From now on, she would be a sign to others that he was alive and near, still sending his angels and working his miracles in the world.

Today Rita Klaus is completely healthy, with no symptoms or aftereffects of multiple sclerosis or any other disease. Her physicians do not know what happened; only that it did. Nor does Rita know why she was selected for this honor. She wrote a book about her experiences and now speaks around the world, witnessing to her journey. Life is not perfect, and troubles occasionally intrude. But from the moment she was spiritually healed, she decided to be completely God's. And nothing will ever change that.[7]

ANGEL OF GOD, MY GUARDIAN DEAR

It is said, and it is true, that just before we are born,
an angel puts his finger to our lips, and says,
"Hush, don't tell what you know."
That is why we are born with a cleft on our upper lips,
and remembering nothing of where we came from.
—RODERICK McLEISH

D ebbie Smith bustled around the family's Wisconsin beach cottage on a beautiful day in June.[8] She and her husband, Tom, had recently purchased the cottage as a weekend and summer getaway, and Debbie was adding homey touches for their three young children, Megan, six; Carrie, four; and Michael, two-and-a-half. Debbie is a postpartum nurse and was then working part-time. She was also thinking about launching a major household-decorating project. Like many young moms, her mind was filled with bits and pieces of life. But the cottage was a respite for her.

"The living room and front porch faced the lake, with a lawn that grew right down to the water," she says. "We had already cautioned the children that if they went even a step off the porch, they had to wear their life jackets." Of course no one was permitted anywhere near the water without Debbie or Tom. To make things even safer, especially for Michael, Tom laid their canoe upside down across the pier that jutted forty feet out into the lake. If Michael attempted to go out on the pier or use the ladder at the end, he would have to crawl over the canoe first. Michael was an active toddler but usually very obedient, and he knew the rule about going outside alone. When Debbie and Tom had taken the children down to the lake the day before, everyone had behaved beautifully. Apparently, the children were adjusting to this new environment and the safety rules it required.

However, that day Debbie wasn't ready to go outside. She was cleaning the bathroom, concentrating on the tub. Yesterday she had given the children a warm bath after they'd come out of the cold lake water, and there was a layer of sand left in the bottom. Before they all went swimming today, she wanted to rinse that away so a shiny and comfortable tub would be waiting. "Can't we go, Mommy?" Carrie asked. Megan was already outside sweeping the garage with Tom as she waited for the others.

"Go, Mommy," Michael echoed.

"You know the rule," Debbie answered, not turning around. "You have to get your life jacket on." Dutifully, Carrie headed for her bedroom, but Michael stayed.

"Want to go out," he repeated.

The sand wasn't going down the drain, and Michael was persistent. "Go and get your life jacket too, Michael," Debbie told him. And as he went out the bathroom door, she added a quick prayer. "Guardian angel, would you mind watching over Michael for a few moments, just until I get this done?"

The prayer was unusual, Debbie admits, because she rarely invoked angels or asked any favors from them. "At that time, I didn't know I could." But she was growing a bit frustrated with all the unfinished tasks and the disarray, and she would take help wherever she could find it! Quiet temporarily descended, and she finished the tub, and then decided to gather all the wet towels from yesterday and start a wash load.

Carrie came into the bathroom and interrupted her mother's thoughts. "Mommy, where's Michael?"

"Carrie, don't step on the floor—it's wet."

"Mommy, where's Michael?"

"He's in his room, honey, getting his life jacket." Debbie started for the washing machine with an armload of towels.

Carrie followed her. "Where's Michael, Mom?" she demanded. "Where *is* he?"

Suddenly, Debbie realized that her daughter had been asking that question for at least several minutes. Carrie asked so many questions—so often—that Debbie had learned to tune her out sometimes. "Isn't he in the house?" Debbie asked. Carrie shook her head. She was wearing her life jacket and her water shoes. Surely, Michael was right behind her with his own equipment.

But he wasn't. Debbie glanced in his bedroom, then quickly checked the rest of the house. There was no small boy on the front porch or the grass. Pushing back a faint feeling of alarm, she went outside. He must be right around the corner. "Mom, where's Michael?" Carrie persisted. Debbie went to the garage, where Tom and Megan were sweeping debris. "Is Michael here?" Debbie asked.

"No. I thought he was with you," Tom replied.

The couple looked at each other. *Where's Michael?*

Fear rising, Debbie broke into a run, going back around the house and toward the lake. There was no one there, and Michael would not have climbed over the canoe. She started to turn away and then, from deep within, she sensed a voice. *Go to the pier,* it commanded. The pier?

Obeying, she clambered over the canoe and ran to the end where the ladder dropped into the water. Michael could climb, but he had never gone *down* a ladder. Had he?

And then the world seemed to stop. Several feet from the pier, floating facedown on top of the wavelets, was the body of her son.

One often hears of people receiving a rush of adrenaline during emergencies, a supersized burst of speed or strength that enables them to perform feats they could not otherwise do. Debbie describes what she experienced as far more than that. Screaming hysterically and calling for Tom, she suddenly felt herself being picked up and thrown into the water. "I felt as if I were wearing strings, and someone else was pulling them. Because it was not me who leaped off the pier, got to Michael, and turned him over. I would have been paralyzed with horror if I had been alone. There was someone else there."

But the horror was with her, too, as she looked at the toddler's grayish face and limp body. *I've lost him,* she though wildly, even as she began mouth-to-mouth resuscitation in the water. *I only have two children now. Please, no, God . . .* "I knew he was on his way to heaven, but I couldn't let him go."

Frantic, she performed CPR, and Tom joined her as they carried Michael through the waves and laid him on the grass. "I worked on him for six or seven minutes," Debbie says. "I couldn't stop working, or praying. Then, all of a sudden, he threw up."

Tom had gotten directions for the nearest medical center—since he did not know how to direct a rescue vehicle to their new neighborhood—and the family sped off. By now Michael was breathing, but he would revive and then faint again. "Pray, girls!" Debbie directed her shaken daughters, who recited the Our Father over and over. By the time Tom skidded into the medical-center parking lot, Michael was alert and speaking. Although the doctors put him through various tests, they found no damage, either physical or mental. Unbelievably, the nightmare was over.

Although Debbie did not want to drive back to the cottage, Tom disagreed. "We're a family, and we have to regroup as a family." And so they did.

"Michael took a very long nap that day," Debbie recalls. "And when he awakened, we asked him what had happened."

Michael admitted that he had not wanted to wear his life jacket. He'd apparently felt certain he could swim without it and had attempted to prove it by climbing down the ladder. "But God was in the water," he announced.

"God was there?" Debbie asked. "What did he look like?"

"I'll draw you a picture," Michael said, and he did. Admittedly, the "God-glob" did not resemble any being Debbie had ever seen. But as Michael pointed out, God was wearing a life jacket. And Michael has never refused to wear his since.

There were no physical effects from Michael's near drowning, and today he is a bright and healthy preschooler. Debbie has had a more difficult time adjusting. "For a while, on our weekends at the cottage, I kept the front curtains closed so I couldn't look out at the lake or the pier." She has also wondered about the extraordinary presence that seemed to be with her throughout this ordeal—never chiding or rebuking, just loving. "From the time I asked Michael's angel to watch over him, he did. The words directing me to the pier, the feeling of being propelled—it had to have been him." Debbie believes that even little Carrie was a messenger. "Her constant questioning was what alerted me that something was wrong."

It is indeed possible to lose a child in a split second of time. But God has given us angels, too, to protect these tiny ones, and parents should ask for their help every day. "I have learned to pray before acting, even in a nonemergency," Debbie says. "To pray before speaking to my children about a problem, to ask the Lord for wisdom, for patience to stop what I'm doing and really listen." As she knows, that prayer may make all the difference.

ANGELS AT THE DOOR

Who can know what tales are told in the whispers of an angel,
Who can see what mighty deeds he does in the name of the Lord?
—DENNIS CARLSON RAGSDALE

⌒⧜⌒

K ay and Johnny Woodhouse were winding up an August weekend with their daughter, son-in-law, and grandchildren at their
summer cottage outside Marion, Iowa. It had been an enjoyable but
unusually stressful weekend, Kay realized, as she packed their
belongings. Johnny had seemed a bit impatient, and that morning
he had complained of being winded on a simple walk. Now that
she thought about it, he had recently had trouble riding a bike up
a hill on one of their outings.

"You're out of shape!" Kay had kidded him. But now she wondered. For the past few months, she and Johnny had been clearing
timber here for their dream house, to be built near the cottage. The
work was strenuous, but Johnny had never seemed worn out. And

today they planned to play golf after lunch with some friends, and he hadn't suggested that they cancel the date. Kay tossed their stuff in the car, kissed her grandkids good-bye, and decided not to worry.

The Woodhouses returned home to Marion just before noon. They were carrying in their gear when the doorbell rang. Kay opened it to two women. They were dressed casually and carried clipboards. Kay assumed they were selling something. "I'm sorry," she began. "I don't have time to speak with you today. We're on a tight schedule."

"We're taking a survey in your neighborhood," the older one declared. "It's in regard to how the Flood of '93 affected people here." The Mississippi River had overflowed its banks in 1993, damaging many cities.

"The Flood of '93?" Kay was baffled. No one had ever asked her about it. Why would anyone want to know now?

"This won't take long." The woman bustled in, somehow taking charge, and set her briefcase on the couch. "We're taking blood pressure readings too," she explained, whipping out a pressure cuff and looking expectantly at Kay.

Well, it wouldn't hurt to have her blood pressure taken. Bemused, Kay sat down and began to explain that the Flood of '93 had presented no real hardship for them. The second woman was busily writing in her notebook when Johnny passed the door, carrying a small television set. "He's the one who ought to have his pressure checked," Kay said, only half in jest. Johnny had seemed very uptight on the way home.

"No way," he answered. "We're going to be late for golf as it is."

"Won't take but a moment," the older woman said, brooking no opposition. She led Johnny to the couch, and, surprisingly, he didn't resist. No one spoke for a moment, and then the woman snapped off the cuff. "You should go down to the hospital and have this checked again," she announced firmly.

"I'm fine," Johnny protested. "C'mon, Kay, we need to grab some lunch and leave."

Both women stood up. "If he were my husband," the older woman said to Kay, "we would be on our way to the hospital *right now!*" She and her helper sailed briskly out the front door, closing it behind them.

Kay was astonished. "Wait!" She opened the door again, full of questions. How could they tell her something like that and simply *leave?* But there were no women on the front walk or moving down the street. No women anywhere. How had they disappeared so quickly?

"Look," Johnny said, lifting his golf bag from the closet, "if it would make you feel better, we can stop at a Care Center on the way home from golf. Let's go."

Kay knew better than to argue. She nodded.

But there would be no golf match today. As Johnny walked to the starter's desk at the course, he suddenly changed plans, beckoning to their friends. "I had my blood pressure taken about an hour ago," he explained casually, "and the woman suggested I go to the hospital. So Kay and I are going to skip golf and get it checked out."

This was news to Kay. And, of course, her independent husband refused to let her drive. She could do nothing but pray—for her husband's health and for safety from potential traffic accidents. By the time they had reached the hospital parking lot, even stubborn Johnny admitted he was having pain.

Kay was sent to the desk to register him, and by the time she got to his examining room, Johnny was hooked up to machines, with several doctors and nurses surrounding him. "Your husband is having a heart attack," one of them told Kay. "Fortunately, he came here in time." *If it had been up to him . . .* Kay wanted to say. Instead, she prayed again, this time for the two women and the perfect timing that had convinced Johnny he needed help.

The next day, Johnny underwent a quadruple bypass, and their four grown children were all there to pray with and support their mom and dad. "That was a miracle—that they all got here so fast," Kay says today. "The second miracle was that Johnny had no permanent heart damage. The doctor said that if he had played golf that day, he probably would have had a massive coronary on the course."

Kay thinks the family experienced a third miracle too. "I checked with my neighbors to see if any of them had been visited at noon on Monday by two women conducting a very odd survey about the Flood of '93—and taking blood pressures at the same time," Kay says. "No one knew what I was talking about."

Kay and Johnny did get their dream house designed and built, and they moved into it in 1996. "We burn wood for our heat, and cut and stack the wood in the spring," Kay says. "Johnny made a dining-room table and a set of bunk beds out of a huge oak that we had cut down. We know that we could not have done any of these things without God's hand to guide us along the way."

God's hand, and some of his very efficient helpers.

BLESSING IN THE SKY

There was a flutter of wings and the bright appearance of an angel
in the air, speeding forth on some heavenly mission.
—NATHANIEL HAWTHORNE, *THE CELESTIAL RAILROAD*

On Saturday, February 20, 2000, the Vuono family boarded a plane for a flight from Tampa, Florida, to Providence, Rhode Island. They were returning home from a visit to Rosemary's mother and stepdad, Marie and Bill, and since it was their second trip to Florida as a family, they were beginning to regard airplane travel as routine. "We had had a wonderful visit," Rosemary recalls. "We are all devout Catholics, so we had even been able to make an unscheduled stop to Our Lady of the Universe Shrine in Orlando, to pray as a family."

The plane had no first-class section, so Rosemary sat in one row near the front, the two children, sixteen-year-old Andrew and ten-year-old Beth, sat on either side of her. On a whim, Rosemary had purchased a large box of animal crackers, which was now stashed in her carry-on luggage. "Just in case we get hungry," she had explained to her husband, Nick, but he had laughed and shaken his head. Women and their purses! Now he sat two rows behind her and across, in the aisle seat. The attendants went through the drill; the plane taxied to the runway and lifted gracefully. The Vuonos settled in to enjoy the flight.

"The first hour was routine," Rosemary remembers. "The children had their headsets on, listening to music, so I focused on finishing my book, Sister Faustina's diary." Sister Faustina was going to be canonized by the Catholic church that coming April, and Rosemary was interested in learning more about her. From time to time, Rosemary glanced back at Nick and noticed that he was talking to the gentleman sitting next to him. All appeared normal.

Then Rosemary noticed that one of the cabin stewards seemed distressed. He was talking to a young flight attendant who looked tearful. Was something wrong?

The captain's voice came over the intercom. "Ladies and gentlemen," he explained, "we have lost one of our two engines, and I'm concerned that we may lose the other one. I have radioed ahead, but was just told to turn back to Tampa. The flight attendants will instruct you on emergency-landing procedures." His voice was calm but urgent. "This situation is serious."

The passengers gasped. Some cried out, and others swore angrily. Rosemary was astounded. But oddly, she felt no fear. Hadn't she just been reading a book about a spiritual woman who had placed all her trust in God? Rosemary was not a saint, but she too knew that this was the only response possible. She glanced at Andrew and Beth. Their eyes were round as saucers, but neither showed evidence of panic.

The flight attendants, some obviously holding back tears, went up and down the aisles making sure everyone had buckled their seat belts. Then they rechecked the overhead compartments. "Could we have some volunteers to help with the emergency procedures?" one asked.

"Nick! You can do it!" Rosemary turned to Nick. He worked for a nuclear power plant and was well trained for emergencies.

"Boy, she can't wait to volunteer me!" Nick joked, lessening the tension among those around him. Some passengers even smiled for a moment. The attendants asked Nick to help with the water evacuation if it became necessary and to block the aisles if people panicked and interfered with the flight attendants. The steward began the drill of crash positioning—feet together flat on the floor, arms up, with wrists crossed on the back of the headrest in front, head leaning down on wrists. He reviewed this several times, with passengers practicing over and over again.

"Mom," Andrew leaned over and whispered, "do you think Nan and Grandpa Bill will find out what happened to us? If we crash, I mean."

"Yes, honey, they'll know." Rosemary smiled reassuringly.

Andrew returned her smile, then reached across the aisle to his father. "I love you, Dad."

"I love you too, son," Rosemary heard Nick reply. Despite the dire drills and the outbursts of weeping or screaming from other passengers, it was surprising, she thought, that her family was so calm. They seemed somehow enclosed in a bubble of peace. "Even knowing we were probably going to die didn't disturb us."

Nick suggested they say a heartfelt Act of Contrition, and after that, Rosemary said a decade of the rosary with Andrew and Beth. She then prayed the Divine Mercy Chaplet (a prayer Jesus gave to Sister Faustina). Finally, she implored God to send his angels to protect the entire plane.

"Mom," Andrew said, looking up at her, "I love you." Rosemary kissed him, then turned to Beth.

"Mom, is it going to hurt?" Beth's blue eyes were shiny with unshed tears.

"No, sweetheart." Rosemary reached for her daughter's hand and kissed her good-bye. Despite the question, Beth seemed serene too. *It has to be the angels, holding their wings over all of us,* Rosemary thought. Scripture passages filled with God's promises to his faithful ones flashed through her mind. She turned and blew a kiss to Nick. His eyes seemed to reflect Rosemary's own thoughts: if God was calling them home, wasn't it wonderful that they were all going together?

The plane began to shake, and the engine noise got louder. There was terror in the screams around her, but Rosemary prayed firmly. The last-minute bargaining with God or worse, the curses of some passengers, were not for her. Would they die as they had lived? She hoped not. "God, you are in control here," she prayed firmly. "Please let your angels hold the plane together, and bring us all to safety." *Our Lady, Sister Faustina* . . . Rosemary invoked the name of all her favorite friends in heaven as she prayed for the crew and passengers. Immediately the plane stopped shaking, and there was a deafening silence. Were they about to crash? *Oh, angels* . . .

Then, the steward yelled, "Brace! Brace! Brace!" The passengers assumed the crash position, and they waited for an explosion. Instead, Rosemary felt a skid, then a hard bounce, and the shriek of brakes. It was the Tampa runway! They had landed.

Rosemary couldn't help herself. "Praise God!" she shouted. Her fellow passengers cheered. Many also wept. The captain quickly shut off the remaining engine, and when he came through the cockpit door, everyone applauded. "I'm so sorry," he apologized. "Please stay in your seats while we wait for instructions. It shouldn't be more than thirty minutes."

Dazed and still disbelieving, the passengers settled down. Soon they were led to a small waiting room in the Tampa airport, where they were told that mechanics were checking the plane. "I'm not getting on that plane again!" several declared. But Rosemary remained unruffled. She noticed that there were several children milling around. Grabbing her carry-on bag, she began to distribute animal crackers—the perfect snack for weary little ones. Once, she caught Nick's eye, and they both laughed. God had apparently provided everything they would need.

In about an hour, the plane was ready to resume flight. A clogged valve had caused one engine to shut down, and mechanics had repaired it. No one explained why, despite the pilot's expectation, the second engine had continued to function. Most of the passengers wearily reboarded, and the trip went off this time without a hitch.

The Vuonos have flown several times since this experience, and they will continue to do so, even though the events of September 11 have changed the way people regard air travel. "I do have a deep faith, and I use all the graces our Catholic faith has to offer," Rosemary says. "I have seen miracles produce faith. And now I have seen faith produce a miracle."

HELPER ON THE HIGHWAY

But if these beings guard you, they do so because they have been
summoned by your prayers.

—St. Ambrose

⤫

Susan Clifford of Leland, Illinois, was diagnosed with diabetes when she was ten years old; her younger brother also had the disease. "Millions live with this chronic and serious illness," Susan says. "But my mom was a positive person, and she stressed each day that our lives could be worse. So I guess I regarded diabetes as a blessing of sorts because eventually it led me to my life's work." As a small child in Catholic school, Susan also learned about guardian angels, and later she named hers Hope. Hope was quite busy, watching over a child with a chronic illness, but Susan thrived. Despite her condition, she became a registered nurse, married a police officer, and had three children.

Life was hectic, but Susan managed to keep her diabetes under control. She used a home monitor to measure her blood sugar several times a day. "That's important because morning insulin can reach its peak around late afternoon, and sugar levels can drop if food is delayed or you are more active than usual." If levels do drop, there are signals that alert a diabetic that food or drink is *immediately* necessary. It's a delicate balancing act but one that people learn to do.

One sunny Sunday afternoon, Susan's teenage son, Matt, asked Susan for a ride to a friend's house. The Cliffords live in a rural setting, with curving roads lined with fields of corn and wheat; they felt that Matt needed more practice time behind the wheel before getting his license. Susan agreed to take him. They had just finished brunch, and since she would be in the car, she decided to go grocery shopping too. She quickly checked her blood sugar, and it was normal. She'd be home well before she needed food again.

"I dropped Matt off and went into town to the supermarket," Susan recalls. "But shortly after I started shopping, something seemed odd."

As she traveled the aisles, the environment seemed to be slowing all around her. "It was taking me forever to choose each item." A faint cold sweat dampened her forehead despite the air conditioning, and she felt a bit dazed, confused. With the part of her brain that was still functioning normally, she sensed that her blood sugar might be low. Maybe a carton of juice would help.

"However, people whose blood sugar drops rapidly don't always process thought in the normal way," Susan says. "They may go on with what they're doing and delay treatment, which makes things worse. It's like a vicious circle." This is what happened to Susan. Moving through the store in a slow-motion haze, she continued to shop for almost two hours. Although she had placed crackers and juice in her cart, it didn't occur to her to actually consume them.

"Confused, I paid for my many groceries, loaded them into the station wagon, got in, and finally downed the crackers and juice. Within minutes, I began to feel like myself." Susan was stunned to discover how much time had passed. Her husband would be worried. She let a few moments pass, just to make sure she was fine, then pulled out of the parking lot and onto the highway.

"I left the front windows open, and after a few moments, I reached into my purse for my rosary," Susan recalls. As a busy mother, she often prayed or talked to Hope while in the car. She was on the first decade of the rosary when she began to feel drowsy. A dreamlike lethargy came over her as she wound around a curve, followed by darkness. How peaceful it all seemed. Were her eyes closed? She didn't know. She didn't care. It was quiet here, quiet and safe. . . .

Vaguely, she heard the sound of tires driving over gravel. But they couldn't be her tires; she didn't seem to be in a car at all. She was floating in space, drifting with nothing around her but this warm, pervading dark.

How long was Susan apparently unconscious? No one will ever know. But her next moment of awareness didn't come until she approached a three-way stop sign in her town, at an intersection not on her normal route, an intersection some twelve miles from where she had slipped into sleep. She was holding the steering wheel, her rosary in her lap, but she was not yet coherent. "I drove past my own house twice before finally pulling into the driveway," she says. Susan ran into the kitchen, where her concerned husband recognized her dazed condition, took a blood check, and gave her some food. Only hours later did she feel well enough to consider what had happened.

Had Susan actually driven that winding twelve-mile stretch at fifty-five miles per hour with her eyes closed? Or had someone else taken over for her, preventing her from causing a terrible accident for herself and others? It had to be Hope, Susan finally decided. Who else could have seen, steered, accelerated, and braked the station wagon but her guardian angel?

"Later, when I drove that route back and forth, I was in awe of the usual high-speed traffic, turns, curves, farm equipment in the road, stop signs, concrete abutments, and children playing," Susan says. "Once I even closed my eyes for a few seconds, and that affirmed my belief that Hope had been in charge. I was left shivering in terror and spilling tears of joy."

Susan believes that she should have followed up the crackers and juice with heavier food before taking to the road. Today she wears an insulin pump, and in her work as a diabetes educator at a nearby hospital, she also trains others with diabetes to use pumps. She shares her own experience as an example of how cautious her patients must be before driving, encouraging them to always check their blood sugar first.

Susan also gives thanks to God for Hope, her life companion. "She is a daily reminder of my faith and the hope that God provides us every day. Angels bring God close to us all. No wonder we love them so much."

DREAM ON

In dreams, the soul transcends the faculties of the body
to hold divine communion with the angels.

—St. Athanasius

"I had the most wonderful message from God last night," a woman told a friend. "But it wasn't true—it was just a dream."

Just a dream? True, dreams are a way of sorting out our unconscious deadwood or releasing daily tension, but God also uses dreams and visions to communicate with his children. The Bible mentions at least seventy events involving dreams or visions; consider Joseph, Jesus' human father, who appears to have been led completely by angelic messages in dreams. In a more modern scenario, at least two of the Pennsylvania coal miners trapped underground in July 2002 recall "seeing" not only glowing lights but also a vision of a beautiful town lying under a starry sky. The scene brought them comfort and somehow reassured them that they would, indeed, be rescued. Discernment is always necessary, but we should pay attention to dreams or visions that seem compelling in some way. Krista Piazza knows this well.

Krista, now of House Springs, Missouri, attended a Lutheran school through eighth grade, and her faith was a very important part of her life. "I especially believed in the power of prayer." As a teenager her church attendance slipped a little, like that of most of her peers, but she continued talking to God and reading her Bible. At seventeen, Krista underwent surgery. A year later, caught up in an abusive relationship, she became pregnant. Because of the surgery's effects, she miscarried at four months.

Perhaps this loss was a wake-up call for Krista. She ended the relationship and rededicated her life to God. Her prayer became more focused too. "God, give me a stronger spiritual life," she prayed. "Bless me with health and with someone worthwhile to love." She believed that anyone's life could be changed, not all at once but one step at a time, each step small but important. One day she attended her niece's birthday party, and one of the guests, Gaetano Piazza, caught her eye. "He was the answer to my prayers," she relates. "We married, and I realized more each day how blessed I was. My only remaining hope was to have a child." The couple was overjoyed when she became pregnant.

But Krista miscarried. She and Gaetano grieved deeply, but Gaetano refused to let either of them become discouraged. Their gracious God would surely hear this most important request. Hope blossomed again during yet another pregnancy. Everything progressed normally, until the fifth month. For the third time, Krista grieved the death of a baby.

"I was devastated," she says. "This was the most painful time I'd ever experienced." Was she being punished for something? No, the God whom Krista had always known was a loving, forgiving God, and she had come to him with the confidence of a child. She could not understand his plan right now. But she knew that his timing was always perfect. She would continue to pray.

In April of 1993, Krista realized she was again pregnant; she was due in January. She and Gaetano held their breath as each week passed. "I was a little paranoid," Krista admits, "especially as I approached the fifth month, the time in the pregnancy when I had lost my last baby." Would the same thing happen again? How could she bear it? "Lord, I'm so scared," she prayed one night. "Please let me know that, whatever happens, you are with me. Send me a little sign, if it is your will."

That night, Krista had a dream. She saw herself giving birth to a child. It was a perfectly healthy girl, a beautiful girl, and Krista could see the infant clearly. Her daughter had pale skin, a round chubby face, and a full head of black hair. "All will be well," someone in the dream was reassuring Krista. "Rest, and be at peace." Was it the voice of her child's guardian angel? Krista was ecstatic and overjoyed during the dream—and she awakened feeling the same way.

Krista told Gaetano about the dream that morning. Gaetano was pleased to see the positive change in his wife. But he wondered what was so unusual. It was normal for pregnant women to have dreams about babies, was it not?

It was, Krista agreed. But such a *specific* baby? And how could she explain the amazing sense of peace that had flooded her spirit, banishing all her anxiety, as she heard those reassuring words? Could an ordinary dream have this effect?

Krista sailed serenely through the next several weeks, even more at ease when an ultrasound revealed that the baby was, indeed, a girl. "I loved feeling her inside me, as if I knew her already, with her round sweet face and black hair," Krista says. On Christmas Eve, as she put final touches on decorations, Krista sent a grateful prayer heavenward. Christmas was her favorite time of year, and this Christmas she had already received the most beautiful gift of her life. In less than a month, their daughter would be here, and what could go wrong at this late date?

But God had another surprise in store, for a few hours later Krista awakened—feeling odd. Could she be in labor? After waiting awhile, Krista phoned the doctor and was told to come to the hospital. It was snowing, and a nervous Gaetano drove through the dark streets as carefully as possible. He was as awed as she. A baby, *their* baby, on this most holy of days!

"Christmas carols were playing in the labor room, and I remember praising Jesus and wishing him a happy birthday again and again," Krista says. But it wasn't until nurses laid the infant in her arms that she realized the full extent of God's faithfulness. "I knew her right away," Krista says. "She had fair skin, a round little face, and a full head of black hair. She was the baby in my dream, the one the angel was protecting."

The Piazzas named their daughter Bianca Noelle Angel, which means "white Christmas angel" in Italian. It has been an apt name, for Bianca seems to understand that there are companions in her world. Once when she was a toddler, she climbed onto the lowest drawer of the dresser in her room, attempting to reach the television and VCR sitting on top of it. Working in the kitchen, Krista heard a crash and came running. Although this situation can lead to severe injuries—and although the TV and VCR were both broken and the dresser lying on the floor—Bianca had completely avoided the crash. She was standing upright, without a scratch.

On another occasion, as Gaetano and Krista finished prayers and were tucking Bianca into bed, the little girl pointed. "Mommy, see the little lights?"

Krista looked. The room was dim. "Where, honey?"

"There, Mommy. And there!" Bianca's face was joyful and excited, as she pointed to little sparkles presumably dancing around her. It was almost as if she recognized the lights, from a time long ago. "This has happened several times," Krista says. "Although I have never seen the lights, they make me feel comforted and cared for, because I have always asked God to let his angels look after Bianca, and I believe he does."

While some dreams are intensely personal, others require that the dreamer become a messenger for someone else, if he or she chooses to accept the heavenly assignment. On a few occasions, Amy Bates of Chesterfield, Missouri, has had such an experience—dreaming about an event that later happened. Often, she has a tingling sensation or a pounding heart, clues that encourage her to take the message seriously. One night in spring of 2003, Amy went to bed early, worn out from a nonstop schedule and caring for three children and a family business.

"I had been asleep for a while when I began dreaming about an acquaintance, Barbara," Amy recalls. "That in itself was strange, because Barbara wasn't really a friend of mine." The two barely knew each other's names, but for the past several years they had occasionally met at grade-school committee meetings or across a soccer field—just two faces in a crowd. "We'd say hi, or wave, and that would be it. Of all the people I could imagine dreaming about, she would be the last."

The dream was fairly intense. There were no clouds, fearful monsters, familiar people, or even a story line, however ambiguous. Instead, a voice was talking to Amy in a rather urgent tone. Within the dream, Amy tried to follow the voice. Apparently, there was a problem concerning Barbara. Amy couldn't get hold of it at first. Then suddenly the message was clear. "You are to call Barbara and tell her to go to her gynecologist," the dream-voice told Amy. "She must go right away."

Amy awoke. The dream still seemed very near, and she was puzzled. Had she heard the message correctly?

And if she had, how could she do this—call someone she barely knew and speak to her about a very personal matter, perhaps even alarm her? Amy shrank from such a task. If this was an angel, why hadn't he just spoken directly to Barbara? And how would Barbara react when Amy told her about it? Would she spread the word that Amy was . . . a bit strange?

Yet Amy could sense that tingling, the feeling that often accompanies these urges for her. "I thought about it again and again that night. It didn't make sense, but if there was a small chance that this request had come from God, how could I say no?" The following morning, as Amy prepared breakfast, she watched the clock. Seven, seven-thirty . . . was it too early to call? Finally, when Amy calculated that the junior high bus had probably left Barbara's house, she phoned.

"It's Amy Bates," she said when Barbara answered. "I don't know if you remember me—we were on a school committee a few years ago."

"Oh," Barbara said. "If you want me to be on another committee—"

"No," Amy said. "I—I want you to listen, just for a moment." Tentatively she explained the dream she had had and repeated the instruction sent to Barbara through her. For a moment both women were silent. What was Barbara thinking? Amy half expected her to hang up.

But Barbara didn't. "You know, this is strange," she mused. "Not too many people know that both my husband and I have been out of work for a while. We have no medical insurance right now, so we've cut back on checkups. I'm way overdue at the gynecologist."

"Maybe this is important," Amy said.

"Maybe. I think I'm going to borrow the money from my mother and make an appointment. Thanks, Amy."

Surprised and relieved, Amy hung up. It had gone far better than she'd hoped. And if Barbara turned out to be healthy after all, well, that was good to know too.

A month or so later, the two bumped into each other again, at a school-band concert. Barbara grabbed Amy's hand and steered her to a private section of the theater lobby. "I had the exam," she said. "They found cancer cells."

Amy gasped. "Oh, no!"

"But I've had treatment, Amy, and I was retested this week, and everything is looking good. I'm well!"

"You are?" Amy could hardly take it in. Barbara's physician had told her that if she had waited even a few months, the outcome might have been critical. But she had received help in time. "If it hadn't been for you, Amy," Barbara said now, tears brimming, "I might not have seen my children grow up."

It wasn't me, Amy wanted to say. She'd had no knowledge of her own. But again she remembered the shivers, the insistent voice, and the command that she wouldn't have considered breaking— and gave thanks.

WELCOME TO PARADISE

The angels came. I saw them there.
They took you up the golden stairs.

—HOPE PRICE, "ANGELS"

When Homer Croft returned from his stint in the Marine Corps, he found a job in Albany, Georgia, to be near his mother and his sister, Ruth. After his mother died, Ruth and her husband, John, invited Homer to live with them. Ruth and John were members of the First Freewill Baptist Church of Thomasville, Georgia. One Wednesday night they invited Homer to accompany them to prayer meeting. "Ruth, do you want the roof to fall in?" Homer asked, only half-joking. His life had been somewhat of a struggle so far, and he was not at all sure that the Lord knew who he was.

Ruth and John assured him that the roof was sturdy, so just to appease them, Homer went along. "I found the Lord that night," he says. And he impressed the pastor, Reverend Floyd Dalton, too, so much so that Homer eventually became an unofficial youth minister for the teenage boys in the church. Reverend Dalton encouraged Homer to share his own difficulties with the boys. Perhaps he sensed that in doing so, Homer might receive some heavenly healing of his own.

People in the church community appreciated this new member and his willingness to take their sons on fishing and camping trips. They also noticed he had a good singing voice, and it wasn't long before one of them gave Homer the phone number of a young woman in town who played the piano and also loved to sing. It turned out to be a perfect match (just as the onlookers probably expected it to be), and Homer and Dene were married about a year later. As an interesting connection, Dene was a cousin of Homer's brother-in-law, John. She also became the piano player for the church.

"Shortly after our wedding, Ruth, John, Dene, and I formed a quartet," Homer says. "We called ourselves The Kinsmen—due to being related to each other in so many ways—and we sang wherever we were invited, all around the tristate area. We did this simply because we loved the Lord." Homer had also become very close to Pastor Dalton. "Even though he eventually was transferred to another church, we never lost touch. He invited us many times to his home for delicious country meals, and this is where I met his mother, who lived in a guest house on their farm." The elder Mrs.

Dalton was a warm and endearing woman. Just being in her presence made Homer feel blessed. When he was eventually ordained a minister and assigned to his beloved Freewill Baptist Church—where his spiritual life had begun—no one was happier for him than Mrs. Dalton.

John and Ruth relocated to Athens, so Homer and Dene found another couple to join them, and they continued their music ministry as the Joyful Singers. They also trained others to sing in quartets or trios—even the senior citizens formed a group. "He who sings, prays twice" goes the adage, and Homer delighted in sending new teams out to churches in the area. The Dalton family continued to keep in touch, even though Mrs. Dalton was now in poor health. Homer often looked back at his life and wondered where he would be if Pastor Dalton had not made him feel so welcome at that first Wednesday-night prayer meeting.

One Sunday morning, Homer felt led to pray for Mrs. Dalton at his service. That afternoon, the Joyful Singers went to perform at a Church of God congregation, a church much larger than their own. First, the congregation sang, and then the church choir. When it was their turn, Dene went to the piano on the platform, and the other three took their places around her. To their right and below them, the church organist arranged his music—he would also accompany them. It seemed like a fairly routine presentation—until the end.

"We had prepared four songs, and the titles of the first three escape me," Homer says. "But I'll never forget the fourth. It was titled 'Beautiful.'" The Joyful Singers got to the last verse of "Beautiful" and were winding up for their conclusion. For some reason, Homer glanced down at the organist—and almost fainted. Lying on the floor right next to the organ was the elderly Mrs. Dalton! She looked quiet and peaceful and was wearing a long white gown.

But how could she be here? Homer thought wildly. She was ill, at home many miles away. His congregation had prayed for her this very morning. Then, as he watched, two angels with short blonde hair, huge wings, and long white robes descended through the ceiling of the church, and flew down to where Mrs. Dalton lay. "I must have stammered in my singing, because I was so astonished," Homer says. And yet, there was no commotion coming from the organist or congregation, no excited pointing or whispering. Was he the only one who could see these beautiful beings?

As Homer stared, spellbound, the angels bent over Mrs. Dalton and gently put their arms under hers. They lifted her as if she were weightless. Then the three flew up and out through the ceiling.

At the same moment, "Beautiful" ended, and the audience burst into applause. Homer's knees were so weak that he doubted he would be able to leave the platform, but somehow he made it back to the front pew. "Dene," he whispered, "did you see them?"

"See who?"

"Brother Floyd's mother, lying on the floor near the organist? The angels?"

"What?" Dene shook her head, clearly confused.

Homer looked at his watch. Exactly 3:00 P.M., and he had probably seen the angels five minutes ago. He would phone Brother Floyd Dalton as soon as he got home. There had to be a reasonable explanation for what he had just witnessed.

When Homer made the call, Floyd's daughter answered. "Dad is at my grandmother's house," she told Homer. "She's critically ill, but here is the phone number. He'll be so glad to talk with you."

A moment later, Homer was speaking to Floyd. "I'm calling about your mother," Homer said.

"She has died," the pastor told him sadly.

"What time did this happen?"

"Just a little before three." It was the answer Homer had expected.

Death is always a loss, but when one is able to assure those remaining that the loved one has gone to heaven, sorrow turns to joy. And so it was for Homer and the Dalton family on that blessed day. "I don't know why I was chosen to see it," Homer says, "but it is only one of several visions God has shown me. Our little church has many angels in its service, and we are grateful for them all."

HEAVENLY MISSION

The capacity to care is the thing which gives life its deepest significance.
—PABLO CASALS

J ack and Mona Barnes, retirees from West Sacramento, California,
parked their car and strolled along a nearby shopping area, soak-
ing up the sun and watching the tourist crowd. When they reached
the door of a favorite restaurant, they turned in without missing a
beat. When people have been married as long as the Barneses, they
sometimes think as one.

The restaurant was crowded as the maître d' seated Jack and
Mona on the covered patio. Mona looked around. It was always
pleasant there. She and Jack both noticed a lovely young woman
sitting alone across from them: light brown hair, about thirty, perfect makeup, a designer handbag draped casually on her chair. The
waiter was serving her lunch, and it looked so delicious that Jack,
normally reserved, leaned across to ask her what it was.

The woman laughed. "It's fajita salad."

"Well, that's my choice too." Jack signaled the waiter.

As the Barneses waited for their lunch, Mona stole another glance at the young woman. Exquisitely dressed, projecting class and wealth, she was obviously a "beautiful person," one of those graced with everything needed for a happy life. Mona imagined the woman in a lavish mansion or jetting off to some exotic location.

Then Mona felt a little signal, a nudge from inside her soul. It was a familiar feeling, one she experienced sometimes as a gentle whisper and other times as a command. She waited, and the message came: "Comfort this woman. She has lost a child."

Oh, no. Mona pushed the conviction aside. She knew perfectly well that the words were coming from her guardian angel. As a member of a Seventh-Day Adventist church, Mona had learned about angels long ago, and she believed firmly in their existence and their purpose as messengers from heaven. Often she had been warned away from accidents or had acted on a request and seen things turn out in a beautiful way. But although Mona was outgoing and social, such things were not easy, especially when they involved a perfect stranger. How could she approach this woman with a memo from God? She wouldn't do it. "Comfort her," the voice prodded. "She has lost a child."

No! Instead of obeying, Mona protested. *There's no reason to think she's lost a child. Look at her—she's laughing at something Jack said.*

The voice was not interested in excuses. "Comfort her. She has lost a child."

Mona was miserable. Her stomach had started to churn. "I looked at the delicious food, but could not eat it because I was too busy arguing with my angel. While Jack and the young woman shared some cheerful comments, I picked at my salad, and resisted." Yes, she knew that God would love her just the same if she refused to acknowledge what was obviously his request. She also knew that all of us were meant to meet one another's needs whenever possible. But this would be so embarrassing! Meddling in someone's life—Mona would be tossed out of the restaurant if the young woman complained. Jack would think she had lost her mind.

But the request continued. "Comfort her."

And Mona's answer was the same: no. She just couldn't.

Finally, she and Jack rose to leave. The young woman was still at her table, enjoying a last cup of coffee, serene and elegant as she had been during their entire encounter. They passed her with a little wave. Mona waited as Jack paid the bill. Her heart began to pound. "You will always be sorry if you do not obey," her angel whispered, more urgent than before. "Go and comfort her. Now."

The battle was over. Mona could resist no longer. As Jack left the restaurant, she turned back and hesitantly approached the table. The young woman turned her lovely face up to Mona, with a questioning smile. Mona took a deep breath.

"God has told me that you have lost a child," Mona said quietly. The woman's expression froze. Mona stammered on. "I—I don't know the circumstances, or if it was a boy or a girl, just that you are grieving, and that God feels you have grieved long enough." Her words tumbled over themselves, coming from some deep place of awareness within her spirit, heaven sent. "You are making yourself ill. God wants you to know that he loves you with all his heart. You are very special to him."

There. Somehow, she had done it. The words hung in the air. Then, suddenly, the young woman rose, threw herself into Mona's arms, and began to weep, deep wrenching sobs. Mona clung to her, stroking her hair as if she was her own daughter. Some of the diners averted their eyes, while others watched, enthralled. "It . . . he was a boy," the woman said through her tears. "I thought God had forsaken me and didn't love me anymore."

"God would never forsake you," Mona told her firmly, more words rising. "So don't you forsake him. Live life his way, and you will hold your baby again. You'll raise him in heaven where no sickness or vileness can ever hurt him."

The woman clung to Mona. Gradually her wild weeping ceased and she quieted. "I needed this so much," she murmured shakily, fumbling for a tissue. "I was praying and getting so desperate. I needed to know that God still loved me."

"Never doubt God's love for you," Mona told her again. She kissed the women and went out, past a group of hovering and bewildered waiters. Later, she would wonder why she never thought to exchange names or phone numbers with this woman in a gesture of ordinary etiquette.

And yet this had been no ordinary encounter. She had agreed to be part of God's plan, she had taken a risk, and now she was happier than she could remember being in a long time.

Jack was waiting patiently in the car, which he had double-parked at the curb. "What took you so long?" he asked her.

"Oh, Jack." Mona sighed, sliding into the seat. "You'll never guess."

WRAPPED IN LOVE

They heard the familiar great shivering of the air, as if wind had passed through a thousand aspens, and the angels were there.
—ETHEL POCHOCKI, *THE WIND HARP AND OTHER ANGEL TALES*

It had been raining all day in Hugo, Oklahoma, and Khristy Sellers really didn't care. Nine months pregnant with her first child, Khristy was eager to give birth. She had planned nothing more strenuous than visiting her friend Amy in the next town for a few hours while their husbands, Roger and Steve, worked together on a truck. "The guys pulled the truck inside the barn," Khristy says, "about a half-mile down the road. The barn was made of tin with, of all things, a telephone inside."

The women stayed at home, played with Amy's two-year-old, and made dinner for themselves and the men. By the time everyone had eaten, the rain was getting stronger, producing occasional hail and lightning. However, for Oklahomans, this was all fairly routine.

"None of us were afraid of storms, because we live in the heart of Tornado Alley, and we're used to wild weather. Many people have underground tornado shelters made of concrete in their backyards. People put chairs, maybe a bed, and some food and water inside."

After dinner, the men returned to the barn. Amy began to fill the tub for her toddler's bath while Khristy lumbered to the couch and flopped down to watch television. The show was continually interrupted by bulletins announcing high winds. "Suddenly the screen flashed red, spelling out, 'Tornado Warning!' The forecaster reported a tornado on the ground in Soper, heading directly toward Nelson." The women froze. That was their area!

"Take shelter, take shelter!" the reporter shouted. Amy phoned the barn to warn the men, but there was no answer. She dialed again, and the phone rang and rang. Where could their husbands go for shelter? The nearest storm cellar was past the house in the opposite direction. They'd either have to run home or lie in a ditch. "Take shelter, take shelter!" She made another phone call, but there was no answer. Outside, the lightning looked like flashing strobes, and hail was pelting the ground. The women's eyes met. Where were the men? What if the tornado had already hit them, and they were hurt?

Khristy impulsively grabbed her jacket and keys to the only car available, her Toyota. "Amy, run! Take the baby to the storm cellar! I'm going to get the guys!"

"No, Khristy!" Amy shouted. But Khristy was already outside, wedging herself behind the steering wheel. She realized how dark the outdoors had become as she started the engine and tried to stay on the gravel road leading to the barn. But it was flooded, making the car difficult to manage. "The rain and hail pounded my car, and the cows had gotten out of the pasture and were blocking the way." She leaned on the horn, which startled the cows into moving, and kept going. At last she saw the barn, but the road leading up to it was rutted and winding. Could she navigate it? Shakily, she urged the car forward.

"The noise was so loud that although my radio was turned all the way up, I could barely hear the announcer yelling to everyone to get out of our cars and find shelter." Tree branches rattled past her as she chugged and bounced down the path, clutching the steering wheel with shaking hands.

All of a sudden, the car hit a deep rut, and Khristy heard a shrill noise. The emergency brake went on and so did all her engine lights. She knew that the engine was going to die—this had happened once before. And there were still several yards to go until she reached the barn. "I knew that I could not make it if I had to get out of my car," Khristy says. "I couldn't run, I could barely walk at this point in my pregnancy."

Gripping the wheel, she prayed aloud. "Lord, help me steer the car. You are in charge of the winds and the earth. Put your protection around me and my baby."

The engine did not die, after all. Instead, as Khristy prayed, the car seemed to reenergize itself. It glided over the water-filled ruts, navigating the remaining curves with ease. "I felt like I was hanging onto the steering wheel, not really driving." As she approached the open barn door, her headlights shone on a flatbed trailer, and the car very gently slid right into it and stopped. She had made it! Khristy dragged herself out of her Toyota and staggered inside the barn.

The men were astonished to see her. They had not heard the phone ringing because of the tremendous noise from the hail hitting the tin barn. "We've got to get you to a shelter!" Roger yelled over the noise. They could use Steve's car. Carrying Khristy, they ran to the car, started it up, skidded around the first curve, and landed in a ditch. No injuries, but another disabled vehicle. There was just one possibility left, a heavy work truck, with a welder and other equipment on the back. Again, the men half-dragged Khristy back down the path and into the truck. Would this nightmare never end? How close was the tornado?

"The roads looked like rivers by then, and the wind was so strong that it rocked that heavy truck," she says. What were they driving into? Where were they? Suddenly, the house loomed in front of them. Holding onto each other, they staggered inside. But this was not a good idea either, for the wind was horrendous. The house seemed to rock on its foundation.

"We can get in a closet!" Roger yelled over the noise.

"No way! We've got to get to the shelter—it's safer!" Steve roared back. Khristy didn't think she could survive yet another trip. But she had to think of the baby. Somehow they staggered back to the truck. Miraculously, it started again, and they headed toward the shelter. But the tornado had apparently changed course. It was right alongside them.

"The ride was a nightmare," Khristy recalls. "Even with the wipers going full throttle, we couldn't see because the rain was coming sideways. There was baseball-sized hail and tree branches of all sizes flying past. Steve leaned over me to shield me in case hail broke the windshield."

And there, finally, was the shelter. The men again helped Khristy to the cellar door amid debris that was flying everywhere. The people below reached out to help her down the stairs as the door slammed behind her. Safe! She could hardly believe it. The journey had seemed to take forever, but she realized that she had left the house on her heroic mission just a short time ago. She looked around. Her neighbors were already assembling blankets and towels for Khristy, to replace her soaked clothes. "What if she goes into labor?" Khristy heard one whisper, and she saw the worried nods. All that running and worrying. But Khristy didn't feel like she was in labor. In fact, aside from being tired, she felt amazingly healthy. And as she looked around, she realized something else.

"Everyone who had run to the shelter had been pounded by hail," she says. "I could see the bruises on their shoulders, arms, backs. But it was dawning on me that I had not been hit once. I had been out in it longer than anyone, running across the fields, the driveways, to the house, to the shelter, but I had never been hit with hail, debris, anything. It was as if an invisible shield was around me and the baby, a shield made of angels."

The next day when the men went to rescue Khristy's car, they received another surprise. Kristy's emergency brake was still stuck in the on position. The car should not have been able to move last night after the light went on. Khristy remembered her prayer and the sudden smoothness of the ride. Had her engine even been running? She realized that she could not have heard it. But God and his angels did not need an engine to transport a vulnerable mother to safety. With God, all things are possible.

As the community later learned, the tornado had been heading for their town but had suddenly zigzagged in another direction, damaging only one roof. No one was hurt, and two weeks later, Khristy increased the population by one, giving birth to a beautiful daughter nicknamed Stormy, who to this day loves going to church.

Was It an Angel?

When you see God's hand in everything, it is easy to leave everything in God's hands.

—Anonymous

⌗⌗⌗

In August of 2003, in Kelowna, British Columbia, a forest fire roared down a mountainside and destroyed 250 homes. More than thirty thousand people were forced to evacuate the area. A few days later, television reporters and cameras followed the distraught residents as they were permitted to return and view the devastation. One woman reached the ruins of her home. At first glance, nothing was left standing but the foundation, the chimney, and a fireplace. She had apparently lost everything.

Then a reporter looked where the woman was pointing. There on the fireplace mantel, sooty but intact, stood her three ceramic angels. The message was clear: she possessed all that really mattered.

Angels are not always so obvious. Much of their activity is performed in silence. We neither see nor hear anything unusual, and if we feel an internal push, it's easy to dismiss as imagination. But there are other times, when the air seems charged with electricity, and somehow we know they have been here.

Did angels have a role in the following incidents? You decide.

Anna Lawik and her young family live in Kielce, Poland, and she often asks angels to protect not only her family but also their possessions. "There are a lot of thieves in our country," she says, and when people are robbed, it can take years to replace the stolen items. One sunny Sunday, the Lawiks impulsively decided to drive to a nearby village. They locked all the doors in their duplex home, quickly put the children in the car, and left. Several hours later they returned. But when Anna looked in her purse, her keys were not there. She began to grow panicky.

Then her husband pointed. "Look!" he said, amazed. Anna followed his gaze. There, dangling from the lock on their fence was her key ring with all the keys intact. "There would have been many people passing our fence that Sunday," Anna says. "Anyone could have taken those keys and stolen everything we had. But no one did." Had angels made the keys invisible? Anna does not know. "But

I don't think it's necessary to see angels," she says. "I have felt their presence many times, and that is enough for me."

Diane called into a radio talk show when the topic was angels. She explained that she had attended a church meeting the previous winter. During the evening, someone announced that a local workman had slipped off a roof and broken his leg. "Let's take up a collection for his family," a woman near Diane suggested. "They'll be needing things he can't provide now." Someone else grabbed a bag and passed it through the rows of chairs.

Diane looked in her purse. She had only a twenty-dollar bill until payday. This was not unusual—sometimes she wished people would take up a collection for her! Nor was this roofer a member of their congregation. And weren't there others here who had more to give?

"Then I felt a firm push, from inside," Diane told the radio audience. "I remembered that I had been trying to develop more trust in God and his angels. I thought about the blessings he had given me. I could work tomorrow, but this man couldn't." When the bag came to her, Diane took a deep breath and dropped the bill into it.

Months passed, the roofer and his family apparently survived; Diane heard no more and promptly forgot about the event. As summer approached, she and her husband realized their vacation fund had grown enough to provide them with a modest trip. On the morning they were to leave, Diane picked up the airline tickets, withdrew $500 from an automated teller machine, added a credit card, and packed everything in her new purse. On the way home, she stopped at the supermarket for some last-minute items. "Absorbed in our plans, I must have left the purse in my shopping cart basket," Diane related. "Because about halfway home, I realized it was missing."

With everything for their vacation inside! Diane drove back to the supermarket parking lot and ran from basket to basket, but there was no purse anywhere. She hurried inside to the service desk. No one had turned it in.

Dianne sagged against the desk, tears filling her eyes. There would be no vacation for them now. Her carelessness had ruined everything. The woman at the service desk passed a phone over to Diane, and she called her husband. No sooner had she begun to explain than he excitedly interrupted.

"I know you lost your purse," he told her, "and some people just phoned. They found it in the parking lot but wanted to make sure that you would get it back. They're waiting for you—here's the address!"

With a shaky hand, Diane copied the directions. All was not lost after all! Moments later, she pulled up in front of a little house, modest but well kept, with several small children playing in back. A young couple was standing at the door, wreathed in smiles. The woman was holding Diane's purse. "Oh, thank you!" Diane burst out as she approached them.

"Everything is there," the husband assured her. "We just didn't like the idea of turning in lost cash. How would you prove it was yours?"

Diane fumbled for the wad and began peeling off bills, but the couple stepped back. "No reward," the young man said firmly. Diane noticed he was wearing a leg brace.

"See, I fell off a roof last winter," the man went on. "I was kind of a rough character—you know the type." He grinned sheepishly. "Skirting the law, a few arrests. But people at a little church near here took up a collection for me." He swallowed. "It changed my whole attitude."

"We'll never be able to repay them," his wife chimed in. "We don't even know who they are. But we're living better lives now— and we can pass on the favor."

Tears blurred Diane's vision. Without the sacrifice of others, this young man would surely have remained embittered and dishonest. She remembered that strange little push and saw herself throwing the last of her money into the bag that night, taking a risk for God, being part of his plan. And she knew it was the best investment she had ever made.

Of course, angels are God's servants, not ours, and we cannot ma-
nipulate them. But we can surely ask that angels go to someone in
distress, surround that person with help or love, and calm the situation. Pope John XXIII frequently prayed for others in this manner. A
teenager who had read about the pope's practice watched a real-life
drama on television one evening, a woman attempting to commit
suicide by jumping off a bridge. Police and rescue workers were
nearby but reluctant to get too close. "I sent angels to that woman,"
the boy reported. "I just asked God to use angels to surround and
comfort her." Within ten minutes, the distraught woman had relaxed
and walked off the bridge into the waiting arms of her family. "What
a lucky break!" one news reporter commented. The teen watching the
program believed it was far more than that.

Shalise Hickman, of suburban Chicago, was very close to her grandmother, Alyce. "My grandfather died when I was seven, so Grandma
spent a lot of time with me." Alyce attended all of Shalise's school
and church events, proudly watching her granddaughter perform in
plays or sing in the choir. When Shalise entered college, Alyce came
for family weekends, along with Shalise's parents. She met Shalise's
boyfriend, decided he would definitely pass muster, and enjoyed

imagining her beloved granddaughter walking down the aisle on her wedding day.

But when Shalise was a college junior, Alyce died. "I was devastated," Shalise recalls. "She had been so special to me, and I had looked forward to many more years with her." Alyce would never see her great-grandchildren. Worse, she would not be at Shalise's wedding. Shalise was heartbroken.

A year passed, and plans for the wedding began. Because it would be held the week before Christmas, the attendants would wear ruby-colored velvet dresses and carry candles within their bouquets of greenery. With seasonal decorations already at the church and reception hall, everything should be exquisite. "I am very emotional, and I was worried about crying through the ceremony," Shalise says. "I knew Grandma would have calmed me down and helped me to be strong." If only her grandmother could be there on her special day.

But wouldn't she? Shalise believed that loved ones never really leave us. But it was so hard to know for sure. Perhaps God could send her a sign that Alyce was indeed near her. "I decided to ask that it snow on my wedding day," Shalise says. Requesting snow in December in the Chicago area wasn't asking for much, she reasoned. Maybe such a little wish could indeed come true.

On that special morning, however, the day was dry, with no snow on the ground and none predicted. As she, her mother, and two of the attendants prepared to leave for their appointments with the hairdresser, Shalise scanned the sky. It was blue and perfectly clear. But there was still time. "Grandma," she whispered, "please be with me today."

The women collected their coats. Just then, Shalise's dad called. "Look at the deck!" Everyone stopped and went to the windows, gazing in awe.

Flakes of snow were suddenly pouring from the sky, coating the brown grass, the dried hedges, transforming the dull landscape into a winter wonderland. The flakes were unusually huge and exquisite, almost as if each had been specially woven. "Let's turn the Christmas lights on," Shalise's mother suggested. "Everything will look so beautiful."

Tramping out to the driveway, Shalise lifted her face to the sky. The flakes floated onto her cheeks and nose, each a lacy kiss from an angel. Was this the sign she had longed for, or just a simple coincidence? "Grandma," she murmured, "is it you?"

And suddenly, as they reached the end of the long driveway and turned into the street, Shalise knew this early Christmas gift was real.

For there was no snow anywhere else. No thick layers covering other yards, no flakes whirling and dancing in the air. No colored lights peeped through webs of white. Everything was drab and dry and ordinary. Everything—except the beautiful winter scene in Shalise's yard, created just for her.

There was no hint of snow at the beauty shop, just minutes away (nor had there been all morning). And when Shalise and the others returned to the house, every trace of fluff was gone. But Shalise was serene throughout her wedding day and has remained so. She knows now that no prayer is too small for God.

CAUGHT!

Oh passing angel, speed me with a song,
A melody of heaven to reach my heart
And rouse me to the race and make me strong.

—CHRISTINA ROSSETTI

J ane and Pete Whiten live in Gainesville, Georgia, but they also have a "relaxation refuge," a forty-acre farm less than an hour's drive away. There, the Whitens, their daughters and sons-in-law, grandchildren, and friends can enjoy animals, nature, and even a western-style village for the children to play in. The Whitens love to entertain, because the farm is meant to be a haven from the rougher pace of the outside world.

One weekend in January of 2000, Jane and Pete brought two of their six grandchildren to the farm, eight-year-old Lendi and her younger sister, Savannah. The girls were looking forward to playing with the animals. "In one holding pen, closest to the house, we had a llama and some small goats," Jane says. "They were going to stay in there with a sheep dog until they were big enough to go to the fenced six-acre area where the larger animals were." On Saturday morning, however, it was snowing, and sleet was also predicted. The girls played indoors, but by late morning, Lendi was bored. "Granny," she asked, "could I visit the animals?"

"Honey, it's pretty messy out there," Jane pointed out. "And if you go over to the pastures, I won't be able to see you."

"Can I just stay in the holding pen?" Lendi persisted. "You could see me there."

"Well, all right." Jane reached for Lendi's coat. It would be all right. Lendi was obedient and wouldn't go farther than she should.

As Jane was putting Lendi's boots on, however, something strange happened. A man's voice spoke into the kitchen, loud and clear: "Look after the child. She could slip and fall, and freeze to death."

Astonished, Jane looked around, but there was no one there. It couldn't have been Pete. He was working on the back porch, building a mud area for shoes, and the voice wasn't his. And, Jane thought, he would have said "Lendi" instead of "the child." The radio wasn't on. Nor did Lendi seem to have heard anything. Puzzled, Jane zipped Lendi's coat and pulled the hood up over her little cap. Had it been her imagination?

"Bye, Granny! I'll stay in the pen!" Lendi waved as she bounced out onto the front porch. Jane went into her bedroom and raised the blinds to watch Lendi. Again, the voice came, startling her: "Watch the child! She could fall and freeze to death!"

What was going on? Jane wondered. Was it some kind of bizarre practical joke? She had no sense of danger at all. She could see the entire pen, even inside the little shed where the animals ate and slept. Lendi had unscrewed the safety latch on the gate, gone inside, and carefully rescrewed the latch. She was happily patting a goat. Over the gate and all around the fence, Pete had put barbed wire so the llama would not jump out. The barbed wire was where it should be. The whole thing was a scene right out of Courier and Ives.

Jane went back into the kitchen to start lunch. "Then I heard the voice again," she says. "It was getting louder and more forceful. I wondered if it might be my brother's voice—he had died suddenly three years ago and had sent me several signs, but it didn't sound like him. This voice was so stern."

As if Jane were not paying attention? Abruptly, she made a decision. Lendi would have to come in, until they could sort out this situation. Jane needed to tell Pete too, although he would probably think she was imagining it all. She went back to the bedroom window, knocked, caught Lendi's attention, and motioned her to come inside. Lendi nodded. It had started to snow heavily again, and she'd be getting wet anyway.

Jane made some sandwiches, still bewildered. A few minutes passed, and she noticed that the snow had turned to sleet. Suddenly the voice came for the fourth time, louder and compelling: "Look after the child!"

Where was she? "Lendi!" Jane ran to the door. It was snowing harder now, and she could barely see through the whirling flakes. Lendi was not on the porch, removing her boots. "Lendi, come in now!" Jane called into the whiteness. "Your mom wouldn't want you to get wet!"

"Granny!" Lendi's little voice floated across the yard.

Why was she still in the pen? "Lendi, come *now!*" Jane called.

"Granny . . . help!"

Frantic, in her stocking feet, Jane jumped off the porch. Then, as she ran through the sleet, she saw her granddaughter. Lendi was caught on the gate, hanging by the back of her coat about eighteen inches off the ground. Her hood was off, her head forced back, catching the full brunt of the sleet. "I could tell that she had been kicking and throwing her arms out, trying to rip the jacket off to free herself," Jane says. "But it wasn't working, and she was getting cold and weak."

Dear God. Jane ran to her and tried pulling her out of the coat, but it wouldn't tear. "Wrap your legs around me, so I can lift you!" she told the exhausted child. With the last of her strength, Lendi did, and Jane was able to unhook her. "I leaned over her to try and shield her from the frozen rain as I carried her to the house," Jane says. "She was soaked and shivering."

With dry clothes, warm blankets, and hot chocolate, Lendi revived quickly. Pete and Jane hung on her every word as she explained what had happened. "The latch was frozen and it wouldn't open, Granny," she said, "so I tried to climb over the gate instead." She had slipped and fallen, getting caught on the barbed wire and hanging helplessly in the air. "I couldn't get any screams out," Lendi explained. "And I couldn't breathe too well."

She could have died, Jane thought numbly. *If she had been out there much longer, with water running into her nose. . . .*

"So Granny, I asked my guardian angel to come and get you," said Lendi. "Did he?"

The voice. Who else could it have been but Lendi's angel, repeatedly trying to warn her about the impending accident? "Oh yes, sweetheart, he did," she told her grandchild. "He certainly did."

"I truly believe angels watch over all of us," Jane says. "But we must listen to them." She thanks God each day that she did.

ANGEL OF HEALING

For certain things are not refused us,
but their granting is delayed to a fitting time.
—ST. AUGUSTINE

⸙

S teve Hooper of Brentwood, Tennessee, had had a routine physical examination every year, during all the years he worked for
Vanderbilt University and when he and his dad opened a small business. He felt he owed it to his wife, children, and business partner
to be as healthy as possible. Every year, "in addition to the normal
middle-aged man's higher blood pressure, the doctor always said my
liver enzymes were not what they should be," Steve says. "But he
never went any farther than that, no extra tests or anything." Because
his physician didn't seem concerned, Steve didn't worry either.

Eventually, Steve's doctor retired. About a year later, Steve
applied for new health insurance and was required to give blood
samples. "In a few weeks, I received notice that my application had

been turned down, due to bad blood results." He immediately made an appointment with a young doctor at a nearby hospital.

"You have hemochromatosis," the doctor told him.

"I have what?" Steve had never heard of such a thing.

"Simply put, it's iron overload, too much iron in your blood," the doctor explained. "A normal person's iron count is in the 50 to 200 range. Your count is 1,620."

Steve was astonished. He'd thought he was taking good care of himself, but this sounded ominous. In addition to eliminating iron-rich foods from his diet, Steve would need a phlebotomy every two weeks. "A phlebotomy is simply a removal of a pint of your blood, until the iron count comes down," the doctor explained.

"What happens if I don't get treatment?" Steve asked.

"Early cancer, a heart attack, or liver damage." The doctor shook his head. "Right now, your liver is in good shape, but . . ."

Steve understood. He went home to tell his wife, Penny. "I was concerned, but not really upset," Steve says. As a faithful Methodist, active in myriad church activities, "I'm a firm believer that nothing happens by chance. God always has a purpose for everything in our lives, whether or not we understand it." Steve was ready for anything that came.

In April, his treatments began. They could last for two or three years, he was told, depending on how quickly the excess iron was removed. However, by July, his blood count had actually increased to 2,250. This was not unusual, his doctor explained. Sometimes the organs actually made more iron to replace what was being removed. He increased the phlebotomies to one each week. What had started as a simple procedure, however, gradually became painful. Steve began to dread his appointments.

By Christmas, the discomfort in Steve's arms was intolerable, and he was unable to sleep for any length of time. "I would wake up in agony, spend hours in prayer, begging God to help me." At about this time, Steve's dog, Socks, began to have convulsions at night. The vet didn't know why.

One night Steve awakened from the sharp stabs of pain, took care of Socks, and then began to pray while Penny slept. He was concerned about his upcoming January blood tests. What if he had a high count again? What would he do? And where was God? Although he prayed constantly, no answers or explanations seemed to be coming his way.

Then Steve looked around. Something was happening. "It started as a faint glow," he says. "Slowly, it got brighter. Then the bedroom was bathed in this dazzling white light." The light did not seem to be coming from any particular place but from all directions at once. It was beautiful, yet frightening. He glanced at Penny, who was sleeping soundly. What should he do?

Then, at the foot of his bed a figure emerged. "It felt masculine, although I could not make out any facial features," Steve says. "He was about seven feet tall, and glowing somehow *within* the glow." The figure wore a white robe and had a pair of very obvious wings on his back. "The wings extended about a foot above his head, almost touching the ceiling." It was an angel, visiting *him!*

The love within the room was almost touchable. Steve felt a warm sensation flowing into his feet and moving gently up the length of his body, as he lay motionless in bed. "Not an outer warmth, but inner, as if the light itself had entered my body." The light was filled with peace and concern, love and healing.

Awestruck, Steve gazed at the apparition. "I am the Angel of Compassion," the figure informed him, not in speech or human language but in a form of telepathy, an inexplicable *knowing*. Comfort seemed to radiate from the angel. He conveyed other information too, but Steve could not comprehend it. What he *did* understand was that he was not to be anxious. His upcoming blood tests were going to show some surprising results.

Gradually, the figure and the light faded. Steve had no idea how much time had elapsed, but his arms no longer ached. He fell into a deep, trouble-free sleep.

As soon as Steve awoke the next morning, he asked Penny whether she had seen or felt the white light that had visited their bedroom. "She had not, and she didn't know what to think of my wild, excited babbling." But during the next month, all of Steve's painful symptoms disappeared.

The blood test results were indeed unexpected. Steve had gone from a count of 2,250 to 17! This was actually too low, and Steve's surprised doctor revised his phlebotomy schedule from once a week to once a month. "This is truly a miracle," the doctor said. "I've never seen a condition like this change so quickly. This should have taken a few years, at least." Socks's convulsions ended the same day, never to return. Was the dog's illness a form of sympathy for Steve? He'll never know.

Today, Steve continues to enjoy good health. He has a treatment once every six weeks, and that seems adequate. He has no pain and is able to do anything he needs to do. "I am a firm believer that each of us is given a guardian angel at conception and that he is with us until the day we are called into heaven," Steve says. "I don't know why I was given the opportunity to look into the face of mine. But I feel led to tell others that God so loves and cares for us that he has sent his Son and angels to live among us, in body and spirit. What a great gift!"

EPILOGUE

We can do no great things—only small things with great love.

—MOTHER TERESA

While reading a magazine in the dentist's waiting room in 1990, I came across a story about a woman named Joann Cayce. She had just received a Thousand Points of Light Award from the first President George Bush, who gave her the award because of her lifelong commitment to the poor. Known as the Mother Teresa of Central Arkansas (despite her Baptist background), Joann, her daughter, Joannie, and Joannie's teenage son, Daniel, apparently constituted a complete volunteer organization. I wanted to know more, so I contacted Joann.

Joann explained that the rural poor have few available jobs and no street shelters, soup kitchens, or overnight programs to give the homeless a warm respite. Even if a family received a box of food, they often had no way to get it home. During the winter, I learned, children sometimes missed school because their shoes had fallen apart. On weekends and summers when schools closed and the federal food programs stopped, some children went without meals. Abused wives needed shelter, elderly people had health problems, and new babies lacked cribs and diapers. Although Joann's headquarters were at her home in Thornton, Arkansas, she actually worked within a sixty- to eighty-mile radius. No two days were ever the same.

Over the years, Joann had built up a donor list of people who collected food, furniture, and other items for her (many just deposited on her porch) and helped her distribute them, but it was apparent that the need was overwhelming and constant. Since I was an incurable garage-sale shopper, I decided to become a helper. Through the next decade, while writing books about heavenly angels, I bought second-hand shoes, baby clothes, and blankets and shipped them to the earthly angels in Thornton. Along the way, I got to know this faith-filled family. Amazingly, they were usually upbeat and rarely judgmental or discouraged. Joannie told me that she considered it a privilege to serve; Daniel confided that his goal was to become an orthodontist so he could straighten needy children's teeth. Even when Joann suffered a stroke, she pushed herself to regain her energy. It was an inspiring connection for me.

In 2001, with the help of some techies, I launched the WhereAngelsWalk Web site, which includes excerpts from my books and a "Story of the Week" from my piles of unpublished readers' accounts. I decided to send these stories to readers on a subscription list, which proved very popular. By December of 2002, more than fifteen thousand people had signed up for the free service, and there are almost thirty thousand on the list now.[9] Many have commented that the weekly mailing was a touch of reassurance in the midst of their often-challenging lives.

On December 14, 2002, as I started to write the weekly story, my thoughts turned to the Cayces. Christmas would be even harder this year since Joann had still not fully recovered from her stroke. December also heralded cold weather, and I began to think of those children and their broken shoes. Slowly an idea grew. What if I told my subscriber list about Joann? At first I rejected the idea: my focus was angels, not fund-raising. If a project of any kind gets too busy, it loses its impact. But the prodding continued (was it the angels?). Impulsively I wrote a new "Story of the Week," explaining Joann's mission and asking interested people to send a pair of socks to her. "It's a gift almost anyone can afford, and it's easy to mail," I pointed out. "If you're already involved in another Christmas project, keep going. But if you are able to do something small, I suspect a pair of socks, even a used pair, would be quite welcome in Thornton." I sent the message off before I could think too deeply about it.

Positive responses came immediately. "I sent your e-mail up and down our block. . . . I put a basket for used sock donations on my porch. . . . Our Brownie troop and their families will be sending socks. . . . This year my staff will buy socks instead of getting me a gift. . . . Could Joann use some gently worn coats too?" Stunned and grateful, I decided to call the Cayces, just in case they began to get a lot of mail. "Socks?" Joann echoed. "*New* socks?"

"Well, yes, there might be several boxes."

"We've *never* had new socks, not in all the years we've been doing this!"

I learned that, as usual, God's timing had been perfect. For just a week previously, Joann had lost her balance while sorting used crayons and had fallen and broken her leg. Now she was in a cast, in a wheelchair, and unable to leave the house. The family had also missed the deadline—for the first time ever—to apply for a donation from Toys for Tots, so the area children would be exceptionally needy this year. I pictured Joann's face lit up in smiles when she saw some socks dancing into her kitchen. But I had wildly underestimated the scope of this project.

For as the packages flowed in, and Joann started to understand the sheer *love* involved, it was all she could do to keep from weeping whenever I phoned for an update. There were bags and boxes everywhere, loaded four deep on the porch, completely filling the little post office branch, piled in Joann's bedroom, and eventually overflowing to the upstairs. The boxes contained socks—ultimately more than twenty-six thousand pairs of them!—but also toys, warm sweaters, underwear (actually the most desirable item), scarves, cases of powdered milk, even cash that went immediately toward the purchase of food. A youth group from Elk Grove Village, Illinois, collected an entire truckload of goods, including—at the last minute—two sacks of toys. Their ministers drove it to Thornton, arriving moments after Joann had run out of toys to give. A man from New York did the same, stopping at prearranged sites across the South to pick up packages. (He was able to outfit a homeless man on the road with donations from the truck and actually shared part of the holidays with the Cayces and their extended family, having nowhere else to go. He said, "It was my best Christmas ever.") A high school student council in Brooklyn ran a sock and gift collection, and a group of Louisiana senior citizens made hundreds of Christmas stockings filled with treats. Employees of large corporations sent samples of their products. People from six countries contributed, including a family from Uganda, itself a poverty-stricken country.

From her wheelchair, Joann unwrapped, sorted, worked the phone, and set up deliveries, aided by the Boy Scouts in the area. At one house in the hills, helpers left a food basket. Later, the mother walked almost a mile to a pay phone, and spent thirty-five precious cents to phone Joann and notify her that someone had made a mistake and included several pairs of brand-new socks along with the food. "It was no mistake," Joann assured her and explained where the socks had come from. The woman broke down and wept. Her children had never owned socks.

Except for one thousand pairs set aside for Christmas 2003, all of the socks and other items were given away by the end of January. Many e-mail subscribers have told me that sending items to Joann will be part of their giving from now on. But there is a greater lesson to be learned from this startling event, the one we have been discussing all through this book.

In Joann Cayce's eyes—and in the eyes of those who reached out to her—the socks were not only a gift, but a symbol of love, a reminder that she is not alone in her work, that others care and are willing to support her. However humble, the socks were a message of comfort. Encouraged by the angels? Certainly, given all the "proddings" so many probably experienced. But put into action by *people*. Angels may whisper to us frequently, but unless we adopt an attitude of listening, of risking, and of doing, life will not change, not for us or those around us.

"When people are more like angels, earth will be more like heaven," one sage pointed out. And she is right. No matter what episodes lie hidden in our murky future, there is no need for fear. For we have *today,* those rich and precious hours laden with potential. One hug, one whispered prayer, one blessing, and even one pair of socks can transform the world. God and his angels will help us do it.

All we have to do is say yes.[9]

NOTES

1. Robin L. Jones, *Where Was God at 9:02 A.M.?* (Nashville: Thomas Nelson Publishers, 1995), 65–66.

2. You can check the song "Hand in Hand" at Dave Allott's Web site: www.holy-smoke.info.

3. Kathleen Treanor, *Ashley's Garden* (Kansas City, MO: Andrews and McMeel Publishers, 2002), 119.

4. Anh Lee grew up to be the author's daughter-in-law.

5. Steve Manchester is the author of *Jacob Evans: At the Stroke of Midnight* and *The Unexpected Storm: The Gulf War Legacy* from which this story was adapted. His books can be purchased online at BarnesandNoble.com and Amazon.com.

6. You can see Terry's beautiful angels on her Web site www.TerrysAngels.homestead.com, or e-mail her for more information at TerrysAngels@mail.com.

7. You can contact Rita about her book or a speaking date at 2 Reedmoor Lane, Cranberry Township, PA 16066, (412) 576-5844. Her book, *Rita's Story* (Paraclete Press), has recently been reprinted.

8. To sign up to receive the angel story of the week, go to www.joanwanderson.com.

9. You can contact Joann Cayce at Joann Cayce Charities, 315 South Second St., Thornton, AR 71766. All donations are tax deductible. The need goes on all year.

RESOURCES

Martha Beck. *Expecting Adam*. New York: Times Books, 1999. Written in novel form, this is the author's true experience of communication with her unborn son while a doctoral student at Harvard and how she came to believe that heaven was watching over her. Mysterious and marvelous.

Beliefnet. *The Big Book of Angels*. New York: Rodale Books, 2002. A grand and well-researched overview of angels in history, religion, and literature, along with true stories of encounters. This book also offers interesting illustrations.

Michael H. Brown. *After Life: What It's Like in Heaven, Hell, and Purgatory*. Goleta, Calif.: Queenship Publishing, 1997. A good commentary about what lies ahead for all of us. Brown, a prolific writer on apparitions, end times, and other fascinating subjects, is also the webmaster of www.spiritdaily.com, an excellent daily roundup of religious news from all parts of the world.

Peter J. Kreeft. *Angels and Demons: What Do We Really Know about Them?* San Francisco: Ignatius Press, 1995. Drawing on the Bible, traditional church teaching, and the church fathers, this is one of the best books ever written on angels. It's presented in a question-and-answer format, with Kreeft's signature humor, and is a perfect start-up book.

Natalie Ladner-Bischoff. *An Angel's Touch: True Stories about Angels, Miracles, and Answers to Prayer.* Nampa, Idaho: Pacific Press Publishing Association, 1998. Warm and charming tales of angelic intervention.

Arthur O. Roberts. *Exploring Heaven: What Great Christian Thinkers Tell Us about Our Afterlife with God.* San Francisco: HarperSanFrancisco, 2003. A collection of opinions about heaven.

John Ronner. *Do You Have a Guardian Angel? And Other Questions Answered about Angels.* Indialantic, Fla.: Mamre Press, 1988. This classic, still relevant, set the stage for the renewal in angel interest in the early nineties.

Peter and Stowe Shockey. *Journey of Light: Healing Our Spiritual Connections.* New York: Doubleday, 2004. A noted film director delves into the need for healing.

MORE ABOUT ANGELS

Angel Collectors Club of America (AACA). A national organization, in existence for more than twenty-five years, ACCA has more than 600 members, with 35 local chapters, and is composed of people who love to collect angels. A quarterly newsletter, *Halo, Everybody,* is also a perk. Membership dues are $20 per year ($25 for members outside of U.S.A.), and you can join by sending your check to Joyce Smith, Treasurer, 234 Granite Creek Road, Santa Cruz, CA 95065.

The Angel Museum, 656 Pleasant Street, P.O. Box 816, Beloit, Wisconsin. Phone: (608) 362-9099. This is probably the world's largest collection of angel figures. More than ten thousand are displayed, including a large collection donated by Oprah Winfrey. Group tours are welcome. Call for hours.

Angels of the World International (AWI). A smaller group than AACA, with similar activities and emphasis on collecting. For more information, e-mail the club's secretary, Barbara Duckworth, at barbs_angels@yahoo.com.

Angels on Earth Magazine. This Guideposts magazine publication offers a bimonthly collection of heart-warming true stories about angels and humans who have played angelic roles in daily life. Subscribe at 39 Seminary Hill Road, Carmel, NY 10512. Fax (845) 228-2115 for information.

I am always interested in receiving angel/miracle stories from readers. If anyone wishes to share, please contact me at:

Joan Wester Anderson
P.O. Box 127
Prospect Heights, IL 60070
E-mail: joan@joanwanderson.com